Medieval Bishops' Houses in England and Wales

Frontispiece: St Davids, aerial view from west of palace, cathedral and fortified gate (Porth y Twr) into close (Ministry of Defence, Crown Copyright)

Medieval Bishops' Houses in England and Wales

MICHAEL THOMPSON

Ashgate

Aldershot • Brookfield USA • Singapore • Sydney

© Michael Thompson, 1998

The author has asserted his moral rights.

Published by
Ashgate Publishing Limited
Gower House
Croft Road
Aldershot
Hants GU11 3HR
England

Ashgate Publishing Company
Old Post Road
Brookfield
Vermont 05036–9704
USA

British Library Cataloguing-in-Publication data

Thompson, M. W. (Michael Welman)
  Medieval bishops' houses in England and Wales
  1. Bishops – England – Residence requirements 2. Bishops –
  Wales – Residence requirements 3. Architecture, Medieval –
  England 4. Architecture, Medieval – Wales 5. England – Church
  history – 1066–1485 6. Wales – Church history
  I. Title
  942'. 03

Library of Congress Cataloging-in-Publication data

Thompson, M. W. (Michael Welman)
  Medieval bishops' houses in England and Wales / Michael Thompson.
  Includes bibliographical references and index.
  1. Bishops—Homes and haunts—England. 2. Bishops—Homes and
  haunts—Wales. 3. Church history—Middle Ages, 600–1500. 4.
  England—Church history—1066–1485. 5. Wales—Church history.
  I. Title
  BR747.T46 1998
  274.2—dc21   98-9974
                CIP

ISBN 1 84014 277 4

Typeset in Sabon by Manton Typesetters, 5–7 Eastfield Road, Louth, Lincolnshire, LN11 7AJ and printed in Great Britain on acid-free paper by The University Press, Cambridge

Contents

List of illustrations

Frontispiece: St Davids, Pembrokeshire: aerial view of palace, cathedral and fortified gateway into the close seen from the west

Preface

My interest in medieval episcopal residences began in 1958 with the remarkable tower base discovered in the excavations on the keep at Farnham, Surrey (Thompson, 1960) and consequent hunting through the Winchester Pipe Rolls, then still at the Public Record Office in Chancery Lane. Acquaintance with the see palace at Lincoln, Durham castle, Lyddington and St Davids did much to broaden these interests. I was anxious to pick a medieval class of person, whose activities were reasonably well documented, the houses of whom had survived in sufficient numbers to illustrate the views I had formed in my books on castles and the hall (Thompson, 1991 and 1995). Bishops' houses seemed an ideal example. Hence the present book, not a catalogue, nor an exhaustive study, but I hope by following certain themes to reach a coherent account of a fairly chaotic subject. The intention is to survey the wood, not climb the individual trees, and over-elaborate treatment with fashionable reconstructions would defeat the purpose for which the book was written.

I have not had an opportunity to see all the buildings in question but fortunately Dr Schofield has covered London examples of episcopal houses, while Anthony Emery's three-volume work on larger medieval houses, of which the volume on the North has already appeared (1996), will furnish descriptive detail of the buildings under examination. This removes the burden of description beyond a minimal level.

Professor Norman Pounds has been collecting information about bishops' houses on record cards over some years, a record that he has most kindly passed on to me. This has furnished valuable guidance on tackling a large and seemingly inexhaustible literature. Dr Phyllis Pobst of Arkansas State University has kindly furnished me with a print-out of Bishop William Bateman's (of Norwich) itinerary prepared for the publication of his register (1996), the first for this diocese, hitherto the only diocese without a published register. I am also grateful to Tim Tatton-Brown for explanations of the excavations on the palace at Canterbury. Dr Charles Coulson has most kindly allowed me to extract licences to crenellate for bishops from his full list. Many others have helped by allowing me to use their illustrations in my figures and will be mentioned in the captions. John Dunbar has advised me on bishops' houses in Scotland and John Newman on the palace at Mathern, Gwent. To all these I am very grateful.

Michael Thompson
Cambridge, 1998

Acknowledgements

For permission to transcribe the 1647 Survey of the archbishop's palace at Canterbury I am indebted to the Librarian of Lambeth Palace Library. For permission to quote itineraries I am indebted to the Canterbury and York Society. I am also indebted to the Bodleian Library for permission to reproduce Tanner MS 217, F. 42 (fig. 38).

I am grateful for permission to reproduce material belonging to the following bodies in the figures specified:

Surrey Archaeological Society: jacket illustration, 47; Ministry of Defence (Crown Copyright Reserved): frontispiece, 98; Cambridge University Air-photographic Collection (copyright reserved): 4, 9, 26, 30, 54, 57, 67, 73, 76; Victoria County History: 6; National Monuments Record: 11, 29, 36, 37, 43, 48, 58, 59, 76; Jan Thorbecke Verlag GmbH & Co.: 14,15; Society of Antiquaries of London: 17, 42, 55; Canterbury Archaeological Trust: 18, 19; Royal Archaeological Institute: 20, 61, 65, 66, 85, 86, 91, 92, 95, 96, 97; British Archaeological Association: 23, 24; English Heritage: 25; Yorkshire Archaeological Society: 27; Society for Medieval Archaeology: 28, 75; Cadw, Welsh Office: 39, 79, 80; London Topographical Society: 46; Newark Castle Trust: 63; Sussex Archaeological Society: 70, 81, 82, 83; Church Commissioners (Archbishop of York): 77; Hampshire Field Club and Archaeological Society: 104, 105.

Abbreviations

Arch.	*Archaeologia*
AC	*Archaeologia Cantiana*
AJ	*Archaeological Journal*
CPR	*Calendar of Patent Rolls*
CYS	Canterbury and York Society
DNB	*Dictionary of National Biography*
EH	English Heritage (Department of the Environment)
EHR	*English Historical Review*
EMB	M. Beresford and H. P. R. Finberg, *English Medieval Boroughs: a Handlist,* 1973
HKW	*History of the King's Works* (1963)
JBAA	*Journal of the British Archaeological Society*
Leland	John Leland, *The Itinerary*, ed. L. T. Smith, 5 vols, 1910
MA	*Medieval Archaeology*
Pevsner	Sir N. Pevsner, *The Buildings of England*, 1951–74
PHFCAS	*Proceedings of the Hampshire Field Club and Archaeological Society*
PSANHS	*Proceedings of the Somerset Archaeological and Natural History Society*
RCHME	Royal Commission on Historical Monuments in England
RCAHMW	Royal Commission on Ancient and Historical Monuments in Wales
RS	Rolls Series
SAC	*Sussex Archaeological Collections*
Schofield	J. Schofield, *Medieval London Houses*, 1995
SRS	*Sussex Record Society*
Stow	John Stow, *Survey of London*, 3rd edn, 1633
TLMAS	*Transactions of the London and Middlesex Archaeological Society*
VCH	*Victoria County History*
YAJ	*Yorkshire Archaeological Journal*

1   *Introduction*

'Bishop', the word being derived from Greek *episkopos*, overseer, was the title conferred on a higher grade of priest who held ecclesiastical jurisdiction over a considerable area, the diocese, a division adopted by Christians from the Roman empire at an early date. There were evidently bishops and presumably dioceses in Britain in the late Roman period, the fourth century AD. However, in this country the mission of St Augustine in 598 was the starting point, spreading from the south-east, for dioceses based on cathedrals – the church with the bishop's throne, the *cathedra* from which the bishop derived his authority. The changes in Saxon times in the dioceses need not concern us; sufficient for our purposes is it that after some shuffling of sees from rural to urban sites in the years following the Conquest the creation of the diocese of Carlisle in 1133 completed the pattern of 21 dioceses (omitting Galloway) that lasted until the Reformation in England and Wales when six more were created in England (Brett, 1975, chap. 1).

A peculiarity of the English bishoprics was that about half of the cathedrals were monasteries served by monks or canons: Benedictine at Canterbury, Rochester, Winchester, Durham, Worcester, Norwich and Ely, and Augustinian at Carlisle. The remaining 9 were secular served by secular canons: Hereford, Lincoln, Wells, Lichfield, York, Exeter, Salisbury, Chichester, London and the four Welsh sees of St Davids, Llandaff, Bangor and St Asaph. In the case of Bath and Wells, a joint see, Bath was monastic, although the bishop transferred his residence to Wells early in the thirteenth century. Coventry and Lichfield was again a partnership with Coventry monastic, the bishop having palaces at both places although he lived mainly at Lichfield from the thirteenth century. The see had earlier been a secular one at St John's, Chester. The extent of the dioceses was more or less fixed but in these two cases the see had two centres. We might expect, then, a total of 24 see palaces although in fact two sees never seem to have had one.

It can be seen in fig. 1 that the variation in size of dioceses was enormous, varying from Lincoln that extended from the Humber to the Thames to a tiny diocese like Rochester that occupied the corner of Kent. More important from a building point of view was the

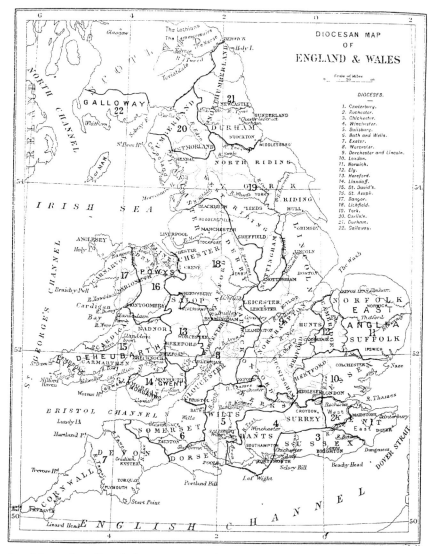

1.   Map of medieval dioceses in England and Wales (G. Hill)

income available to the bishop: rich, £2500–4000 a year (Winchester, Canterbury, Durham); comfortable £1500–2500 a year (Ely, York, Lincoln, Bath and Wells, Exeter); tight, £750–1500 a year (Salisbury, London, Worcester, Norwich, Hereford); poor, £100–750 (Carlisle Rochester, Coventry and Lichfield, Chichester and the Welsh dioceses) (Heal, 1980, 40).

These figures are derived from the *Valor Ecclesiasticus*, the great survey at the Reformation of monasteries and cathedrals. There are earlier figures from the Domesday Book or the *Taxatio ecclesiastica* of the late thirteenth century, or later ones from the sale of episcopal lands by parliament at the time of the Commonwealth (Tatham, 1908) but all indicate the same sort of distribution of wealth.

The money derived from temporalities and spiritualities, or secular and ecclesiastical as we would say. The first was far more important for all except the poorest sees. When the dioceses were created land was given or bequeathed to the institution, the cathedral, but by the Norman Conquest or soon after, the capital was divided into two: one to support the prior and convent (the *mensa*) in the monastic cathedrals, or the dean and chapter in the secular cathedrals, and the rest to support the prelate (Howell, 1982). Only when the bishops enjoyed full rights over their manors could they freely use the resources accruing to them to construct houses.

At the Reformation there were estimated to be 640 manors belonging to the bishops, Winchester having 75, Canterbury 66, Durham 62, Ely 50 and so on down the line. The manors normally lay within the bishop's diocese, but in some cases outside, particularly with the archbishop of Canterbury. Not only did a bishop's resources come principally from his manors but he lived most of the time in houses on them, so they are central to the whole story with which we are concerned (fig. 2).

Manors could be in demesne, that is farmed directly or let out which was less usual. In the former case there had to be buildings to house the bailiff who was running the property, but when did a house qualify as an episcopal residence? A rule of thumb is: when it had a chapel. There are said to have been 168 such episcopal residences at the Reformation (Hembry, 1978).

There were two other types of residence that did not lie at the centre of a wealth-producing unit but, quite the reverse, were places for spending money. The first of these was the see palace near the cathedral, the seat of the bishop's authority. The second of these was the London house acquired from the thirteenth century by nearly all bishops for attending parliament and doing business in the capital, not to mention for social life. In this book the subject will be dealt with in the sequence see palace, London house and manor house, giving priority to castles when the house took this particular form. It is not a catalogue although there is a 'working list' at the end of he book arranged by dioceses with the

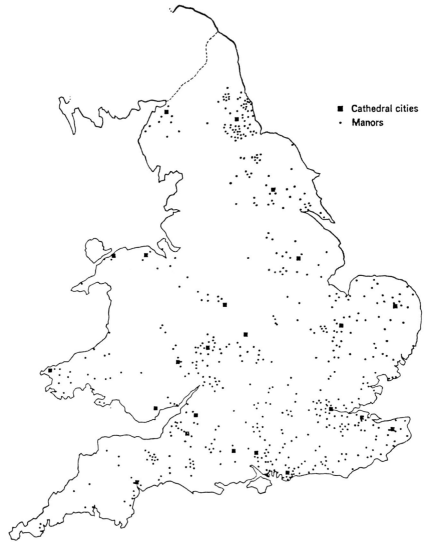

2.   Map of cathedrals and episcopal manors in England and Wales during the middle ages (F. Heal)

houses in this order (without, it is hoped, any serious omissions) that can be used for reference.

Readers may be puzzled by the word 'palace'. In an amusing article it has recently been demonstrated that in north Italy bishops adopted the term 'palace' for their houses in the cities in the tenth and eleventh centuries to establish their superiority over the houses (or palaces) of similar form being erected by the Communes (Miller, 1995)! 'Palace" originally referred to the house of Augustus on the Palatine in Rome and was gradually adopted by other emperors, in particular by Charlemagne. It became a general term applied to any royal residence, and in due course to episcopal residences. It is not commonly used in medieval sources for houses on the manors and there is something a little absurd about applying it to houses that often compared unfavourably to laymen's houses. In the twelfth century it seems to be applied particularly to hall blocks, so Prior Laurence at Durham speaks of two palaces at Durham castle (Thompson, 1994), or the Winchester annalist speaks of a sort of palace, quasi-palatium, of Henry of Blois (Luard, 1864, ii, 51), presumably meaning a hall range. The sensible compromise seemed to be to adopt the term palace for the bishop's residence in the close and otherwise use house, unless there was a strong convention, as in Lambeth Palace. The contemporary word for the London house was 'inn'. There is no real doubt about a castle, no doubt for the medieval scribe nor for ourselves, a house in which the defensive features completely overshadow the domestic ones.

i Contemporary sources

The wealth of contemporary sources referring to bishops is very great indeed and we certainly cannot even remotely understand the physical remains without them. If attention is turned first to those that emanated from the bishop himself there are two kinds of account that are of especial value.

Household accounts, for obvious reasons very rarely surviving, give a day-to-day record of expenditure of a very intimate kind: food, drink, travel, transport, messengers and so on. They were first used by Webb (1853) to describe the journey on visitation of Richard de Swinfield, bishop of Hereford, in 1289–90. They have been used very successfully by Aston in her book on Thomas Arundel, bishop of Ely (1373–88) (Aston, 1967). Kitchen accounts are usually destroyed but we must hope more will come to light.

The second type of account is manorial, that is recording receipts and expenditure from tenants and farming on the bishops' manors. The main set are those of Winchester, starting or surviving with many gaps from 1208 to beyond the middle ages, at first in rolls (hence Winchester Pipe Rolls) and from the mid-fifteenth century in book form. They are fair copies derived from fuller accounts for each manor and then stitched together at the top. The first two have been published and an English translation of the roll for 1301–2 (Hall, 1903; Page, 1996). They grew enormously in bulk in the later thirteenth century. It is items of expense that interest us: parks and fishponds so skilfully used by Roberts (1986); buildings notably exploited at Bishops Waltham by Hare (1988), at East Meon by Roberts (1993) and Southwark by Carlin (1985).

It may help the reader to illustrate my own use of this source for dating the great brick tower at Farnham (Thompson, 1960a). I stumbled on the entries accidentally in the books 1470 to 1475, those for 1471 and 1474 having been lost. The entries record the nature of work although sometimes mixed with other work shown by asterisks in the accompanying table. One can almost watch the tower grow from foundation to roof (fig. 3)! As the tower had previously been attributed to Foxe (1501–23), even to the extent of seeing his initials on the building, the proper attribution to Waynflete (1447–1486) was of especial interest. Not all cases are quite so neat; the identification of existing buildings with those referred to in the accounts can be very difficult.

	1470 £.s.d.	1471 £.s.d.	1472 £.s.d.	1473 £.s.d.	1474 £.s.d.	1475 £.s.d.
Foundations	5.8.0*					
Demolition of old work	11.1.0*		3.19.4*			
Bricks:						
Making & firing	29.13.9					9.16.4
Carriage to castle	1.12.6		1.5.0	0.7.6		1.2.8
Laying on new tower	12.16.8		9.13.4			30.0.4
Dressing or laying dressed bricks				2.7.6		
Carpentry			18.6.8*	4.5.10*		24.9.0
Window & door fittings			10.3.11	9.8.8		
Roof (tiles, lead, gutters)						7.2.3*

* includes cost of other work

3.   Farnham castle, Surrey: the great brick tower erected by Bishop
William Waynflete in 1470–5 (M.W. Thompson)

From the thirteenth century onwards a record was made in each
see of important documents, ordinations and so on, which is known
as the bishop's register. Many have been published. As many have
the place of execution of the document it is possible to work out the

bishop's movements, often for the whole of his episcopacy, creating an 'itinerary'. As he was almost continuously on the move these can be of great interest. Examples will be given below.

Chronicles, sometimes emanating from a monastic cathedral, can be an important source, particularly in the twelfth century. Most of our knowledge of the great castle builders comes from this source. William of Malmesbury actually devoted a volume to the activities of bishops (Hamilton, 1870).

Crown sources are also very important particularly because bishops themselves played a major part in government. As far as buildings go, the licences to crenellate on the back of the Patent Rolls are as important for bishops' buildings as for those of the laity.

This does not exhaust the documentary sources for bishops' houses but it will give the reader an idea of the wealth of material. Court rolls are another important source.

ii   What did a bishop do?

A bishop's duties fell into two categories: the running of his estates and household and his ecclesiastical duties as a bishop. The first could be a full-time job for a conscientious bishop to judge by the advice of Grosseteste to the Countess of Lincoln (Oschinsky, 1971, 388–409). The chief officer on that side was the steward. On the ecclesiastical side the chief officer was the chancellor with other legal officers who accompanied the bishop on his travels.

Bishop Praty of Chichester (1438–45) has left a register (Deedes, 1905, 85) that has six divisions denoting the bishop's duties :

1. Admissions, institutions, collations, registrations of clergy
2. Mandates from superiors: pope, king, archbishop
3. Election of abbots and priors
4. Visitations
5. Memoranda and noteworthy acts
6. Ordination

Much of the work was that of a superior personnel officer or headmaster or inspector. Careers depended on him. His courts dealt with adultery, divorce, family feuds and so on. He was not a popular figure although a respected one, rather like a senior administrative civil servant today.

One function not recorded in the registers is the holding of synods (Cheney, 1941). Theoretically all the clergy of a diocese were summoned twice a year to an assembly in the bishop's hall for 'inquiry, instructions, correction, law-making'. In practice only a fraction of the clergy could attend. It lasted a day, a second day for deacons. It issued statutes, a sort of diocesan law code. In France it has given its name to the main first-floor hall of the évéche, the *salle synodale*. In England perhaps only Puiset's decorated hall on the first floor at Durham (fig. 107, p. 160) has a feeling of the synod or chapter house.

Both sides of his work, visitation and supervision of his manors to maintain his income, required continual travel by the bishop within the diocese. The inspection in visitation could not be done sitting in one place and equally the vigilance required to check fraud or falsification of accounts had to be done on site. As Grosseteste makes clear, one could not simply rely on the steward but had to master all the aspects of the episcopal estate.

What is surprising on looking at the registers is how infrequently documents were signed at the see palace: some bishops seemed hardly ever to go there. We have seen how the property of the institution was divided, more than half going to the bishop who enjoyed more or less a freehold on his manors while he lived. Once he entered the close he was in the domain of the prior and convent or dean and chapter: there was bound to be hostility and suspicion or tension at the best of times. Kathleen Edwards (1949) writing of secular cathedrals described it thus, speaking of the chapter:

> They were so sensitive of these rights and privileges that bishops usually found it advisable to stay away from their cathedral cities as much as possible. The dean and chapter came to be regarded as the rulers of a kind of autonomous ecclesiastical republic within the diocese.

This is perhaps exaggerating since at Chichester the relationship seems to have been better. However, there was always tension that could end with violence as it did under Bek at Durham (Frazer, 1957, chap. 8).

A long letter or memorandum of Grosseteste to the dean and chapter at Lincoln gives us an insight into the relationship (Luard, 1864, 257–83). It sets out the very special qualifications that allowed him and him alone to carry out his important duties of visitation. No doubt the object was placatory but it is difficult to think of a document more likely to raise the hackles of the recipient.

The result is important in the study of episcopal houses in that the old buildings found in the see palace remained largely unaltered. No one who has been to Wolvesey can fail to have been impressed by the remarkable survival of the twelfth-century buildings throughout the middle ages.

The later developments of secular domestic architecture such as formal courtyards or lodging ranges are rarely found. No doubt the constriction of the close raised difficulties but one cannot help feeling that if the bishop wanted to reconstruct the palace he would have done so. The buildings were required for courtrooms, special feasts and so on but the bishop if he had to use them did so for as short a period as possible. All his duties in connection with patronage, confirmation, ordination and so on could be exercised from one or two important manor houses. Normally, therefore, one or two of his manors situated not too far from the see became his main residences and the nearest thing to home that he had. The great late medieval builders like Wykeham, Waynflete, Morton, Warham and Wolsey did their major work on the manors, not at the see palace.

When did this manorial way of life emerge? It could really only start when the property had been formally divided between the bishop and the institution. In spite of the absence of registers it was clearly the norm by the twelfth century and perhaps goes back to pre-Conquest times – cf. Eadmer's reasons for Anselm's residence (Southern, p. 71).

iii   Travelling

The most convenient way to illustrate the travelling is to take four six-month periods from the itineraries constructed from the registers. The first is Grosseteste himself, bishop of Lincoln, for the second half of 1240 (Davis, 1913, xi):

July 13	Fingest, Beds	House
	28–9	Banbury, Oxon	Castle
August 3	Arningworth?	
September		
	16–28	Lyddington, Rut.	House
October 7	Keten (?Ketton)	
	21	Nettleham, Lincs	House
November		
	9–16	Buckden, Hunts.	House
	22	Biggleswade, Beds	House

	30	London	
December			
	2–3	London	
	12–15	Buckden, Hunts	House

The next is Archbishop Winchelsey of Canterbury in the first half of 1299 (Graham, 1952, xxv):

January			
	6–24	Mayfield, Sussex	House
	29–30	Otford, Kent	House
February			
	2–16	Chartham, Kent	House
	24	Canterbury	Palace
March			
	14–20	Lambeth	Palace
	20	Lewisham	House
April	1	Gillingham, Kent	House
	4–5	Horton, Kent	Nr Canterbury
	4	Charing, Kent	House
	25	Maidstone, Kent	House
	27	Malling, Kent	Abbey
May			
	1, 3	Otford	House
	8	Maidstone	House
	9–16	Lambeth	Palace
	16, 19	Croydon, Surrey	House
	23	Malling	Abbey
June			
	12–19	Otford, Kent	House

The third half-year is from the itinerary of Henry Woodlock, bishop of Winchester in 1312 (Goodman, 1940, xxv):

July	1	London	
	25	Esher, Surrey	House
	26	"	
	28	Newark, Surrey	
August	1	Southwark	House
	5–8	Marwell, Hants	House
	9–10	B. Waltham, Hants	House
	17	Farnham, Surrey	Castle
	2–23	Hackington, Kent	
	23–29	Southwark	House
September			
	1–14	"	
	15	London	
	23	Kingston	
	26	Esher, Surrey	House

30	Wargrave, Berks	House
October		
3–10	Esher, Surrey	House
11	Kingston, Surrey	House
12–21	Esher, Surrey	House
November		
4–5	Southwark	House
8	London	
9–22	Southwark	House
December		
1–20	"	
20–30	Esher, Surrey	House

The following is from a print-out kindly supplied by Dr Phyllis Pobst for William Bateman, bishop of Norwich, in 1354:

January		
7	Terling, Essex	House
12	London	
22	Kevedon, Essex	
24	Ipswich	House
30	Norwich	Palace
February		
9–21	Hoxne, Norf.	House
March 4	"	
15–16	London	
April		
24–27	Terling, Essex	House
May 16	Eccles, Norf.	House
17–19	Hoxne	House
27	Weybourne, Norf.	
30	Massingham, Norf.	
31	Gaywood, Norf.	House
June 1	"	
6–12	Hoxne, Norf.	House
16	Norwich	Palace
17–29	Hoxne	House

The travelling continued all the year round regardless of the seasons. No clear tendency for the visits to London can be discerned, perhaps the autumn and winter being more favoured.

A table constructed by Roberts (1993, 477) in connection with his work at East Meon showed when the bishops of Winchester between John of Pontoise and William of Wykeham conducted business at certain manors from which I have extracted five to show the variation in use from one episcopate to another of different manors.

House	John of Pontoise 1282–1304	Henry Woodlock 1305–16	John Sandale 1316–19	William Edendon 1346–66	William of Wykeham 1367–1404
Bishops Waltham	12	37	6	77	352
Bitterne	15	44	2	4	0
East Meon	1	18	2	1	0
Highcleere	2	104	3	59	150
Wolvesey	144	17	5	59	120

The fluctuations in the preferences of bishops for different manors is very evident from Highcleere, Bitterne or even Wolvesey palace. At Bishops Waltham we can see the increasing importance attached to it by Wykeham which was even more marked under Cardinal Beaufort when it became the most cherished of the Winchester houses (Hare, 1988).

Many details of travelling are known from the few surviving household accounts. The body that moved from one place to another might consist of 50–100 people. The bishop and a small group of senior officers rode on horseback. The furniture, linen and other movables preceded in wagons. In the story of St Hugh of Lincoln the pet swan at Stow Park knew when he was coming since the wagons arrived first and the bird could then make its way to the hall to greet the bishop (Douie and Farmer, 1962, 104–9). Whether the remainder of the household rode on the wagons or had to walk is not clear but probably the latter.

Apart from his manors the bishop could usually put up at monasteries within the diocese, over many of which he enjoyed rights of visitation. There was also an obligation on parish priests to provide accommodation although this was usually commuted for a cash payment, 'procurations' as they were called.

The life of a bishop if he carried out his duties well was by no means one of idleness: the responsibilities were considerably greater than those of a modern bishop. His inquisitorial and patronage powers made him a respected but not popular figure. The incessant travelling must have been irksome if not physically uncomfortable, and since there was no age of retirement it was unpleasant for older men. Few like St Hugh rode with their eyes turned heavenward but few bishops had been Carthusians. The medieval bishop almost literally dropped in his tracks.

2   *Castles by the cathedral*

The whole concept of a cathedral, the church with the bishop's throne at the heart of his diocese, would have made it anomalous and indeed absurd for the bishop to fortify his residence adjoining the source of his authority. With the possible exception of Gundulph's tower at Rochester, which may have been a campanile (Hope, 1900; Tatton-Brown, 1984) rather than a keep, no English bishop constructed a castle by his cathedral. In Wales Llandaff is an exception due to special circumstances in the principality. Among abbots that of Peterborough (not yet a cathedral) stands as a scandalous exception due to the motte and bailey north of the church (Thompson, 1994).

As part of the establishment of his authority William the Conqueror erected castles in most of the important Saxon towns in the country either himself or by an authorized earl. As a rule the castle was thrown up at the opposite end of the town to the cathedral, presumably to avoid any clash of authority, as at York, London, Norwich and Canterbury, with a few exceptions like Worcester. This appreciable distance between the two would have made the castle an unsuitable place for the bishop to live in. The cases where the bishop did acquire a permanent or usually temporary residence in the royal castle arose because of special circumstances that have to be discussed individually: Durham, Lincoln, Old Sarum and possibly Ely.

i   Durham

Durham was a very different case from the other sees. It was very vulnerable from Scottish attack, particularly at this time in the eleventh century, and although the position is not quite clear it had enjoyed a special status even before the Conquest. The king ordered the castle to be built when he was in the north (Thompson, 1994) and this was presumably carried out by Earl Waltheof. However, the earl came into conflict with the king and was executed in 1073, the whole of his powers and authority including the castle passing to the bishop. Durham remained in an anomalous position, being

4. Durham: aerial view from west of castle and cathedral with the Green between: former part of town until cleared by Bishop Flambard. The motte and two hall ranges are clearly visible in the castle (Cambridge Collection)

excluded for instance from the Domesday survey, the Prince bishop enjoying an autonomy quite unknown in the other dioceses. Physically the castle was separated from the cathedral by part of the town until the houses were cleared away by Bishop Flambard (1099–1128) to form that huge area of mown grass and parked cars that separates the two today (fig. 4). His predecessor, Bishop William de St Calais (1081–96), had rebuilt the cathedral and replaced the canons with Benedictine monks.

The river Wear has created that spur of high ground known today as the 'peninsula', the castle transecting it transversely at the northern end with the cathedral lying similarly transversely across it further south. The existing castle that the bishop received was presumably simply a motte and bailey of standard shape which still dominate its present form. All the later structures, apart from those made when it had become part of Durham University in the last century, are due to the bishops. The mound of the motte is crowned with a modern structure, the successor to several alterations including no doubt one or two stages of wooden superstructure. The remarkable feature of Durham castle is the twelfth-century poem by Prior Laurence describing it (Thompson, 1994; Raine, 1839), quite unknown for any other English castle. At that date, c.1140, there was a square structure on top, probably a sort of private retreat for the bishop, surrounded by a stone wall, a shell keep. We know that Bishop Fox (1494–1501) was proposing to carry out alterations there before his transfer to Winchester so it seems likely that the top of the mound was inhabitable throughout the middle ages (figs 5, 7, 8).

Prior Laurence refers to the chapel and the two 'palaces' in the bailey below. The chapel of c.1100 is one of the outstanding features at Durham on account of the highly decorated capitals of the columns of the vault. It has lost its upper floor, two-storeyed chapels being *de rigueur* in episcopal houses, perhaps with a wooden roof, although the columns referred to by Laurence must be those we see today. The two odd features of the chapel are its lack of an apse and its projection into the motte ditch as if indeed it were earlier. The two 'palaces' of Laurence are not what we see today since in their present form they must be later. There were probably ranges in the same position, that is on the north and west, and the foundations discovered by Martin Leyland (1994) suggest there was also a range on the east side (figs 7, 8). The present ranges are mainly Puiset (1153–95) on the north with the fine decorated door-

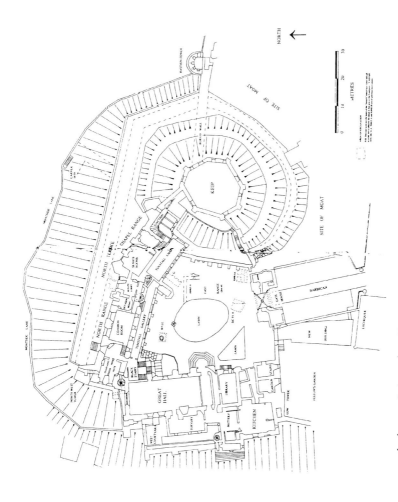

5. Durham castle: general plan as it is today. Excavations were made east of the Lawn where an early range was found (Martin Leyland)

17

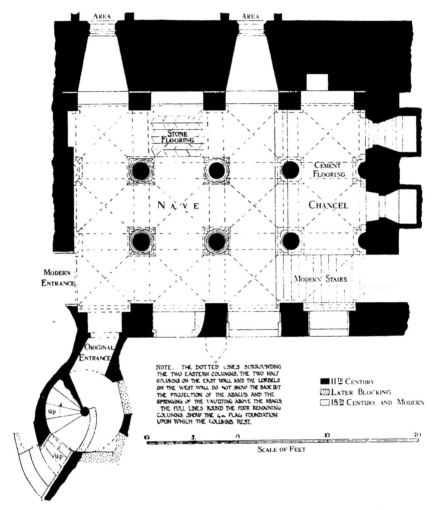

6.   Durham castle: the presumed undercroft of the chapel with three pairs of piers with highly decorated capitals to support the vault (*VCH*)

way on the ground floor and decorated gallery on the first floor (figs, 106, 107: pp. 159, 160), and on the west thirteenth century raised over an undercroft. The west range was extended south by Bishop Fox and contains the kitchen. It served as a courthouse with presidential seats at either end. The width of the hall suggests that its span required a single aisle on one side. Leyland has made the interesting suggestion that the famous gallery with Norman decoration at dado level on the first floor of the northern range (the

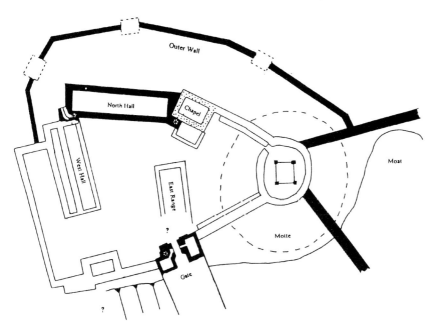

7.   Durham castle in the time of Bishop Flambard (1099–1128) as drawn by Martin Leyland

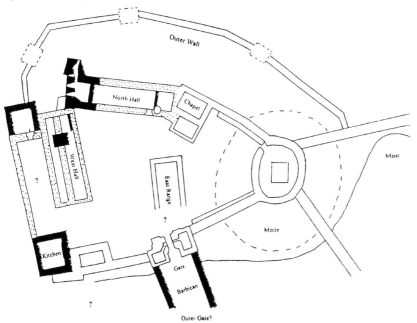

8.   Durham castle in the time of Bishop Puiset (1153–95) showing his additions according to Martin Leyland

'Constable's Hall'), was intended to be seen from the ground like a sort of clerestorey in a church. The only comparable decoration at Angers in France runs round the first floor of the hall, *salle synodale*, of the bishop's palace, and this is surely more likely at Durham, the arcade recesses over the bench providing seats in chapter-house fashion. This, like many other matters at Durham, requires resolution and goes far beyond what it is possible to describe here.

ii   Lincoln

There is perhaps some analogy between Durham and Lincoln in that there was a strategic consideration in transferring the see from Dorchester on Thames to Lincoln in view of the Scandinavian threat. The large number (60) of knights' fees of the bishopric would furnish knights in emergency. Remigius came over with the Conqueror in 1066 bringing supporters with him, apparently with the promise of a bishopric as his reward (Thompson, 1998). He was installed as bishop of Dorchester on Thames but the see was transferred to Lincoln in 1072. The construction of the cathedral began at once in the south-east corner of the upper Roman town, that is opposite the castle in the south-west corner of the town, which had no doubt been constructed by this time. There was evidently a deliberate intention to create a processional way between the two, as indeed the elaborate treatment of the west end of the cathedral suggests (fig. 9).

The steps up to the motte top of a castle were normally against the curtain wall but at Lincoln the steps to Lucy's tower, as the structure on the motte is known, are in the middle, not adjoining either curtain. This suggested a change of plan: if the line of the steps were extended on a straight line then the line reached the north-east corner tower known as the Cobb Hall tower. It looked as if this was the original east side of the castle before an annex on its east side was added to give the castle its squarish shape, and this annex had its own motte now with Observatory tower on top (fig. 10). Bishop Bloet in c.1110 received permission to construct a gate, presumably the existing one by the buried Roman west gate to form an exit (*exitus*) out of the castle, surely meaningless unless he was living in the castle. It is suggested that bishops Remigius and Bloet lived in the castle with a gateway on the east side, so constructed that it faced the west end of the cathedral, the gate forming the

9. Lincoln: aerial view from the west showing the castle with Lucy's tower and prison on the 'annex', the Observatory tower with the west end of the cathedral beyond. The bishop moved from the annex to the Roman east gate, north of the chapter house and then to the site south of the south transept where the Alnwick tower between the halls can be seen (Cambridge Collection)

LINCOLN   CASTLE

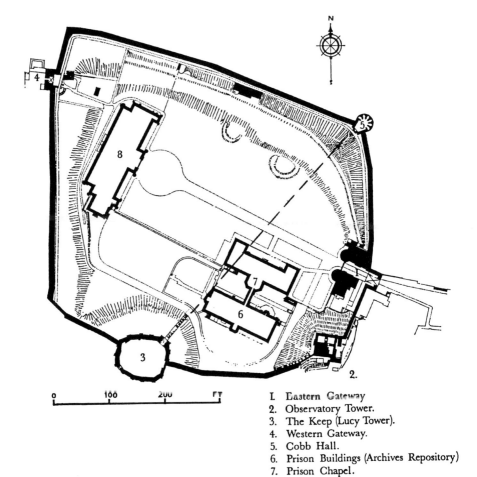

1. Eastern Gateway
2. Observatory Tower.
3. The Keep (Lucy Tower).
4. Western Gateway.
5. Cobb Hall.
6. Prison Buildings (Archives Repository)
7. Prison Chapel.
8. Assize Courts.

10.   Lincoln castle: plan showing with a broken line the assumed course of the east side of the original castle (M.W. Thompson)

other end of the processional way. There was of course no close wall or Exchequer Gate at that time to obstruct the route, since the whole area enclosed by the Roman wall constituted a close or precinct, as it were.

Bloet's successor, Bishop Alexander (1123–48), the great castle builder, was authorized to live in the Roman east gate tower north of the cathedral, moving in effect from the castle to his own keep. This did not last long, for soon after he was authorized to break through the south wall of the upper Roman town to create an entry (*introitus*) to the cathedral from a house he might build there. This is presumably when the palace on the present site was created and the east hall may well go back to that date.[1] This third palace where the ruins exist will be discussed in the next chapter.

iii   Old Sarum

Old Sarum, north of Salisbury in Wiltshire, is an extremely interesting case of movement of the palace to three different sites but for quite different reasons. There is a huge more or less circular earthwork on the hill above the later city of iron age origin which served the Romans as their *Sorbiodunum* and in its turn became the city of Salisbury after the king had planted a ringwork castle in the middle. The cathedral of the see was erected to the north west of this. The first bishop's palace was built to the north of this and linked to the church at its east end by a sort of cloister. This was a rather crude six-bay hall with central entry and later service annex, that is a pre-standard type hall. It could have been the work of either Osmund (1078–1099) or Roger (1102–39). That was the first palace; Roger then acquired the adjoining royal castle and built within a courtyard house of the type with which his name is associated. This was the second palace (fig. 11).

This remarkable style of building will be discussed later (p. 88) where the better example at Sherborne, Dorset is described. At Old Sarum there may have been royal buildings already there that prevented free design, and there obviously was a pre-existing enclosure. Four ranges enclosed a small courtyard with a keep in the north east projecting from the enclosure as a kind of mural tower. Some or all of the ranges were two-storeyed (it was not level ground) and half the southern range at its east end was occupied by a two-storeyed chapel, St Margaret below the vault and St Nicholas above. The west range was designated the 'hall' by the Commission[2] and measuring 15 by 7 metres internally is bigger than the north range, 13 by 5 metres internally, but the latter adjoins the kitchen. If the latter is the hall (frater) then the claustral origin of the design is evident although not as apparent as at Sherborne where double-storeyed chapel and hall face each other across the 'garth'.

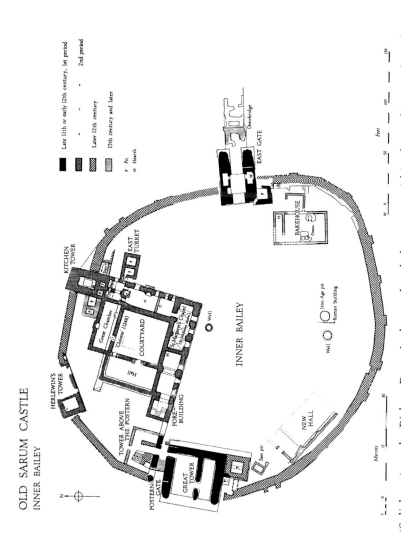

OLD SARUM CASTLE
INNER BAILEY

Late 11th or early 12th century, 1st period
"   "   "   "   "   2nd period
Later 12th century
13th century and later

P Pit
H Hearth

HERLEWIN'S TOWER

KITCHEN TOWER

EAST TURRET

TOWER ABOVE THE POSTERN

FORE-BUILDING

Great Chamber

Cloister (1246)

COURTYARD

St Margaret's Chapel (originally Kitchen)

HALL

Well

POSTERN GATE

GREAT TOWER

Saw pit

INNER BAILEY

NEW HALL

Well

Iron Age pit

Roman building

BAKEHOUSE

Ovens

H

EAST GATE

Drawbridge

Metres

Feet

11. Old Sarum (Salisbury) castle. Bishop Roger's claustral-style house set within the earlier royal castle (RCHME)

24

In the 1220s the city moved down into the valley to form the modern Salisbury with its regular street plan. Bishop Richard Poore (1217–28) started the new cathedral and with it the third palace.[3] Much of this survives and has recently been studied by the Royal Commission. I am inclined to think that Bishop Poore's hall was over the vault in what is called the 'solar', like Bishop Jocelyn's hall at Wells with which it is broadly contemporary, and the development took a rather similar course. However, this is a matter to be discussed later (p. 51).

iv   Ely

Ely did not become a cathedral until 1109, its diocese being carved out of an oversized Lincoln. Bishop Hugh of Northwold (1229–54) is recorded to have built the palace south west of the west front[4] but where the bishops lived in the 120 years before this is not clear. Adjoining the abbey to the south by the river is a fine motte and bailey known as Cherry Hill (fig. 12) and, although no doubt it was royal in origin the bishops had a castle, probably this one, and lived in it (Brown, 1959, 267). However, there is some doubt about the number and situation of castles in the Isle so it is not certain.

v   Llandaff

The last site at Llandaff, Glamorgan, on the outskirts of Cardiff differs from the castles hitherto discussed in that it was built by the bishop himself just south of the cathedral overlooking a steep slope. It is nearly two hundred years later than the others of which we have just spoken but must qualify as a castle rather than a palace (fig. 13). It has recently been surveyed by Johns (1974) and the Welsh Royal Commission.[5] It is a fairly regular quadrilateral in shape with a gatehouse with rectangular spurred towers of the type met on the Welsh borders and dating a little before 1300. The south-west tower is square and the south-east one round, while at the north-east corner the two-storeyed hall projects outwards to serve as a tower, recalling the design of the later Llawhaden castle of the bishop of St Davids. The hall with two storeys and unequal division to create a chamber has a spiral staircase housed in a projection. Seeing the two-storeyed hall acting as part of the de-

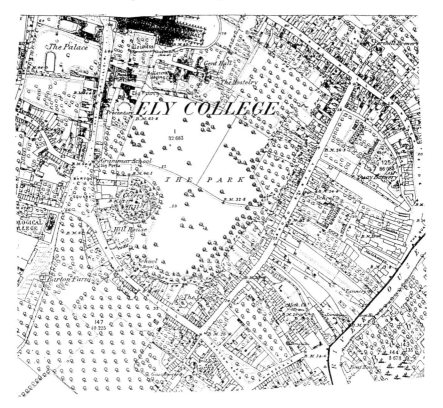

12.   Ely: first edition Ordnance Survey map showing relationship of Cherry Hill motte and bailey castle to the priory and later palace west of the cathedral

fences surely gives us a clue as to why this form continued in use as the favoured form and was not replaced by the native English form on the ground floor. One might use the same argument in Scotland or its border.

Its construction is attributed to Bishop William de Breuse (1266–88). The motive for its construction in this form is not hard to find since it coincided with the height of Llywelyn the Last's greatest extension of power to near Cardiff (his forces burnt Caerphilly while under construction). It lies outside the close insofar as one can speak of this at Llandaff.

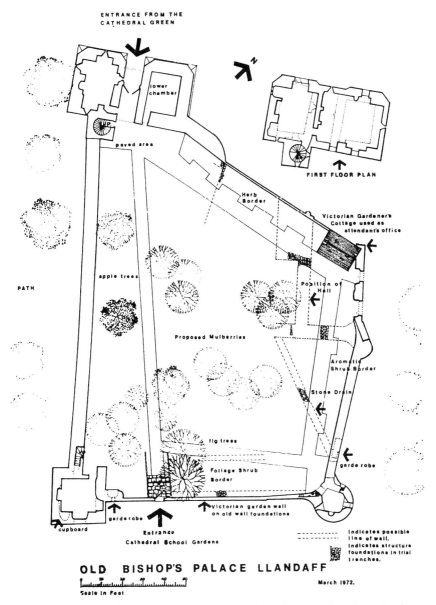

ENTRANCE FROM THE
CATHEDRAL GREEN

lower
chamber

N

paved area

FIRST FLOOR PLAN

Herb
Border

Victorian Gardener's
Cottage used as
attendant's office

apple trees

PATH

Position of
Hall

Proposed Mulberries

Aromatic
Shrub Border

Stone Drain

fig trees

garde robe

Foliage Shrub
Border

garde robe

Victorian garden wall
on old wall foundations

cupboard

garde robe

Entrance
Cathedral School Gardens

---------   Indicates possible
---------   line of wall.
▨   Indicates structure
             foundations in trial
             trenches.

OLD   BISHOP'S PALACE LLANDAFF

Scale in Feet

March 1972.

13.   Llandaff castle, Glamorgan: plan by C.N. Johns. Note how in this late 13th-century castle the hall projected as a tower at one corner. Cf. Llawhaden in fig. 79 (p. 121)

Notes

1. See Thompson (1998); there was a further authorization or confirmation in 1157.
2. RCHME, *City of Salisbury*, ii, 15, 22.
3. RCHME (1993), *Salisbury: the Houses of the Close*, 53–83.
4. *VCM, Cambridgeshire*, iv, 82–3.
5. Further information kindly supplied by RCAHMW.

3   *See palaces*

i   Continental bishops' palaces

The instances where a bishop lived in a castle at the see have just been described: if castles were something entirely new brought in at the Conquest so, equally, the cathedrals themselves and the houses occupied by the bishops were replaced by new buildings that, so far as we know, differed entirely from what had been there before. Apart from Wulfstan at Worcester the entire native episcopacy had been replaced by Normans a few years after the Conquest. We have no knowledge of what a Saxon bishop's palace might have looked like, although its most prominent feature was probably a tall ground-floor hall with attendant smaller buildings. What replaced it was quite different, based on the norm on the Continent, a single two-storeyed block containing many of the ancillary elements.

The author has discussed elsewhere how a two-storeyed hall block became the norm on the Continent by the tenth century (Thompson, 1995, chap. 3), the lead perhaps being given by the German emperors. The changes from Carolingian to Ottonian palaces have recently been discussed by Zotz (1993) with valuable maps and figures. In north Italy where the term 'palatium' was adopted for the bishop's house by the tenth to eleventh centuries (Miller, 1995) sufficient examples survive, perhaps best at Como, to show that the normal episcopal palace consisted of a two-storey range with open arcade on the ground floor and subdivided internally on the first floor into chamber and hall by a cross wall. This may have a tower at one end and the ground floor is normally vaulted. This type would stem from or at all events be related to German imperial palaces of the Goslar or Magdeburg type, where the palace consisted of a single hall block (*Saalbau*) vaulted over the ground floor. It will be appreciated that the design differs fundamentally from the barn-like English hall.

In France where, although no bishops' palaces are earlier than the twelfth century, the survivors of that period give a fairly good idea of what a Norman prelate elected to an English see after 1066 would have wished to live in, so far as local skills would have allowed it to be built in the same form. They have been described by

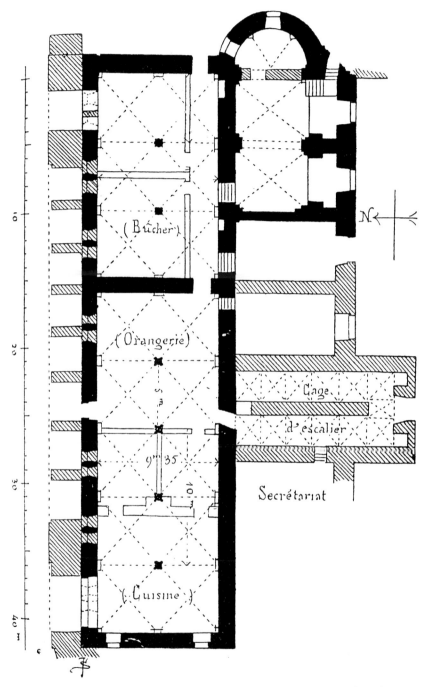

14.   Meaux, Seine et Marne: Plan of vaulted ground floor of 12th-century bishop's palace; note subdivisions for hall, chamber and chapel above (Héliot)

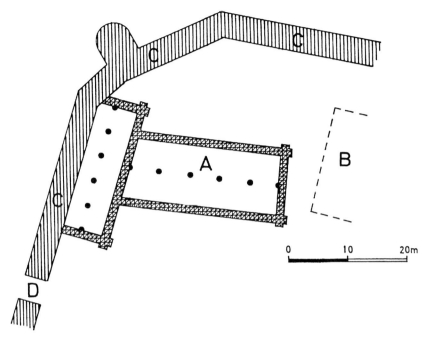

15. Angers, Maine et Loire: The bishop's palace: A, hall over; B, cathedral transept; C, Roman town wall; D, town gate. A may be an enlargement from original hall on left (Héliot)

the late P. Héliot (1976). Without exception they are two-storeyed blocks vaulted at ground floor level and subdivided for a smaller room at each level (fig. 14). There are some differences between north and south France, whether the chapel is absorbed into the range, and in both areas the large external stair of the secular hall block is absent (Esquieu and Pradalier, 1996). At Angers a larger range has been added at right angles to a smaller range as the responds shows, very much recalling the usual English development made by simply erecting a larger hall and retaining the older one as a private suite for the bishop. The simple plan at Meaux (fig. 15) with its chapel shows the basic principle, while the reconstruction by Viollet le Duc (fig. 16) of Archbishop Sully's palace at Paris (destroyed in 1831) shows a late twelfth-century version, directly linked (like Norwich) to the cathedral (Mortet, 1888).

For the study of the English sees it is important to appreciate two points: the block was always two-storeyed and vaulted over the ground floor; there was only one range, chamber and hall being

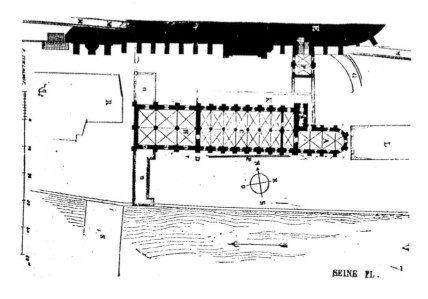

16.   Viollet le Duc's plan and reconstruction of the 12th-century archbishop's palace destroyed in the 1830s. Note how hall and chapel on first floor are linked directly to Notre Dame

created by internal division, normally a transverse wall. Much of the controversy about 'chambers' is due to the misunderstanding that in this type of block it was not a separate building but contained within the range.

ii   Benedictine abbots' houses

As we have seen, nearly half the cathedrals were Benedictine monasteries and the bishops appointed by the Conqueror were often monks like Lanfranc, Anselm and Gundulph. The same period saw also a considerable influx of monks or monasteries closely linked to Continental orders like Cluniacs. It was part of the cultural infusion from across the Channel.

In his study of the abbot's house at Battle Abbey, Brakspear (1933) compared six abbots' houses (fig. 17). It will be seen that they filled the west range of the cloister adjoining the western alley. The hall is always on the first floor over a vaulted undercroft with spinal arcade. The chamber and chapel were created by internal division at the north end. The whole arrangement is clearly just a version of the Continental hall block that has just been discussed. At Westminster, Battle and Gloucester the first-floor hall was later replaced by a ground-floor one following standard English practice as happened with bishops' houses.

The position of Lanfranc's palace parallel to the west range of the cloister suggests that he was trying to follow Benedictine practice as closely as his position of archbishop of Canterbury would allow. The matter will be discussed below.

iii   See palaces

The see palaces can be considered chronologically but before doing so there are a couple of general points to be made. Was there any regular position for the palace to be placed? The answer must be no, with some qualifications. At Lincoln the bishop lived first due west, then north east and then south of the cathedral (p. 20). The first position lined up with the western façade of the cathedral and was perhaps an ideal for a secular bishop. With a monastic cathedral there was a precedent for the abbot to live in the west range and this evidently influenced Lanfranc at Canterbury.

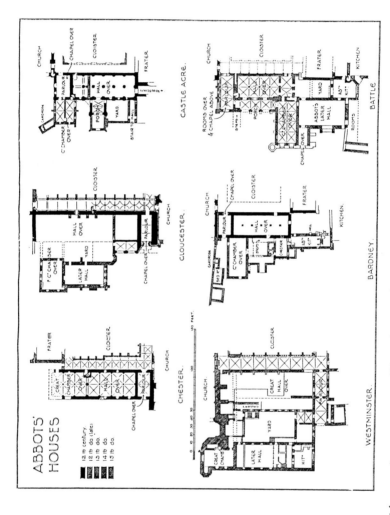

17. Six abbots' houses in west range of Benedictine cloisters: note subdivision of chamber from hall and replacement by ground-floor hall in some cases (Brakspear in *Arch.*, 83)

34

One can perhaps say that a roughly westerly position in the outer court was preferred (Canterbury, Worcester, Rochester, Ely, Norwich but not Wolvesey!), but with the secular cathedrals, where there was no obstruction by cloister and no outer court, an easterly situation was sometimes preferred (Exeter, Salisbury, Lichfield). There is no hard and fast rule. The requirement for separate outside access to avoid close jurisdiction was certainly a primary consideration in the choice.

It seems to be very common both at see palaces and manor houses that the primary hall was superseded by a larger hall, sometimes soon after but sometimes long after its original erection, but now retained with a different function, as private quarters for the bishop. Whether this was due to the increasing size of the household or to provide better provision for a courthouse it is not possible to say (Mertes, 1988) but it will be discussed further (p. 125). Here it is sufficient to draw the reader's attention to this so that it will come as no surprise when encountered.

It is convenient to start with Canterbury where recent excavations have shed a flood of light on the original palace (Rady, Tatton-Brown and Bowen, 1991). It has been suggested that the block or range running parallel with the west range of the cloister, parts of which were incorporated into a modern building, represents Lanfranc's original hall block (fig. 18). It was two-storeyed with a vaulted ground floor, but at right angles to this is another two-storeyed range of the same width but much longer with a free-standing kitchen near its western end. It is known from excavation that it was vaulted over on the ground floor although this range has not been fully explored. It impinges on the north tower of the west front of the cathedral, which suggests that it was an afterthought or addition made when the earlier range left no choice but to put it there. The west façade of a Romanesque cathedral was its main show front, not to be obscured under normal circumstances (fig. 19). Eadmer refers to this building (Bosanquet, 1964).

The murder of Becket in the cathedral was described in several accounts that are contemporary or almost so set out by Professor Barlow in his life of Becket with some guidance on recent discoveries by Tim Tatton-Brown (Barlow, 1986). The fullest of these accounts is in French and has two lines (5183–4) (Walberg, 1922) of special interest to us:

Mais le seneschal ent devant els encontre
E il vint encontre els tresqu'al pie del degre

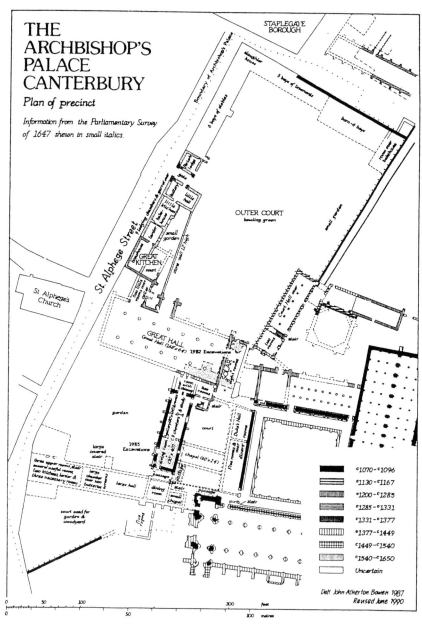

THE ARCHBISHOP'S PALACE CANTERBURY

Plan of precinct

Information from the Parliamentary Survey of 1647 shown in small italics.

18.   Canterbury: site of excavations on archbishop's palace west of cloister by the Canterbury Archaeological Trust

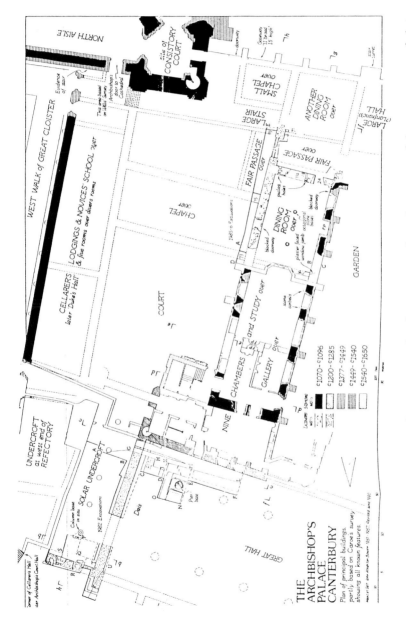

19.   Canterbury: more detailed plan of excavations by the Trust on the palace west of tŀe west range of cloister

37

This must be a clear reference to the external stair of the block which the steward descended where he kissed and greeted the knights, unaware of course of their real intentions. It is a nice piece of confirmation of an upper floor and a very rare reference to the external stair.

The palace was still only two-sided, L-shaped and open on the north. This side was filled early in the next century by the eight-bayed aisled great hall of the new standard design, as I have called it. Sadly, it was destroyed at the time of the Commonwealth and all that survives is the north porch. It has however been the subject of research in the last few years (Rady, Tatton-Brown and Bowen, 1991) that has recovered some of the column bases and that has shown what a significant building it must have been. The contrast between this and the earlier ranges, which must have looked as if they had just come over from the Continent, is very striking. Its upper end linked up with Lanfranc's first hall, now presumably the chamber or at all events the archbishop's private quarters, following the sort of change of which we have spoken. In spite of the paucity of visible remains the recent work at Canterbury has been very revealing (cf. the 1647 Survey on p. 163).

The bishop of Rochester was regarded almost as a suffragan of the archbishop of Canterbury but in the eleventh century the see was filled by the remarkable Bishop Gundulph (1077–1108), brought over from Bec, whose name is particularly associated with the construction of the White Tower in the Tower of London. He was responsible for construction of the palace apparently on an extension of the precinct created by breaking through the Roman wall to the south west of the cathedral. Only a single block survives of what had become a courtyard in the later middle ages (Hope, 1900; Tatton-Brown, 1984). Although no early detail survives, it seems clear that in origin it is similar to the sort of hall blocks we have been considering.

Lincoln is in some ways the classic bishop's palace. It is the third site for the palace (p. 21), built after permission had been given to break through the southern wall of the upper Roman town just south of the south transept of the cathedral (fig. 20). It consists of two halls with the fifteenth-century Alnwick gate tower between them. There could hardly be a greater contrast between the halls. The east hall is set over a massive undercroft, partly rock cut, with a division on the floor above creating a chamber at the southern end. There is a later chapel at its north end. It is evidently a hall block of

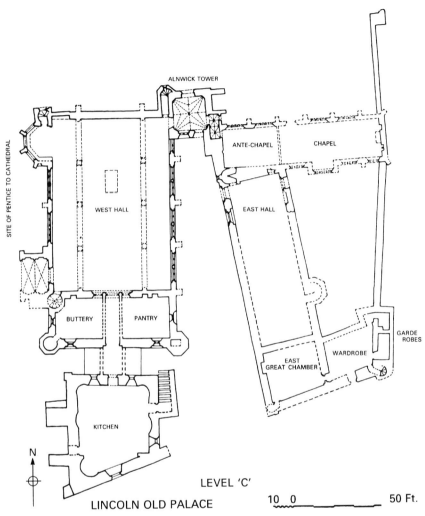

20.   Lincoln: plan of bishop's palace showing both halls, Alnwick tower, chapel and kitchen (Faulkner)

Continental style. The west hall, albeit very ruinous, is a ground-floor aisled hall with central hearth, three fine service doors at the southern end, the central one leading to a magnificent kitchen reached across a bridge (figs 21, 22). There was a chamber on the first floor over the service bay (now converted to a modern chapel). There is no chamber wing at the upper end and it seems fair to assume that the east hall took on this function when it was superseded by the

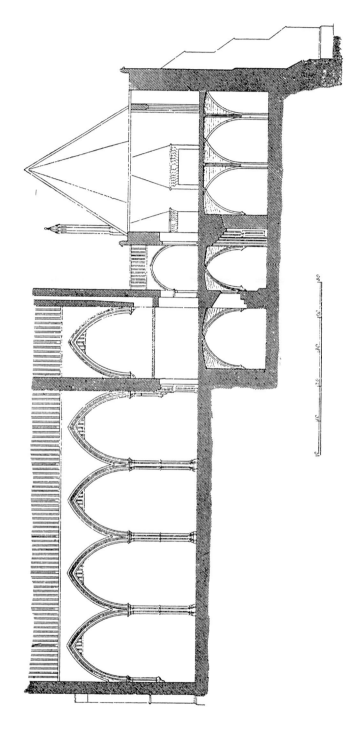

LINCOLN PALACE. LONGITUDINAL SECTION OF GREAT HALL, KITCHEN AND DEPENDENT OFFICES.

21. Lincoln: longitudinal section through the west hall and kitchen with reconstructed arcade and roof over kitchen. Note three levels in fifth bay and bridge to the kitchen (Hodgson)

22.   Lincoln: west hall in bishop's palace showing three service doors and site of piers and central hearth marked out (A.E. Thompson)

west hall. The west hall made wide use of Purbeck marble and had a porch on the west side. It is thought to have been started by St Hugh but only finished by Hugh of Wells, the architectural detail fitting in with the two written references (Faulkner, 1974). The sequence recalls that at Canterbury.

At Norwich the palace was set by Bishop Losinga (1090–1119), the first bishop after the move from Thetford, against the north wall of the nave between the fourth and fifth bays from the transept. It is aslant to the nave wall which cuts off its south-west corner as though the nave were later than the palace (fig. 23). It is the only case where there was direct access to the nave through a doorway at

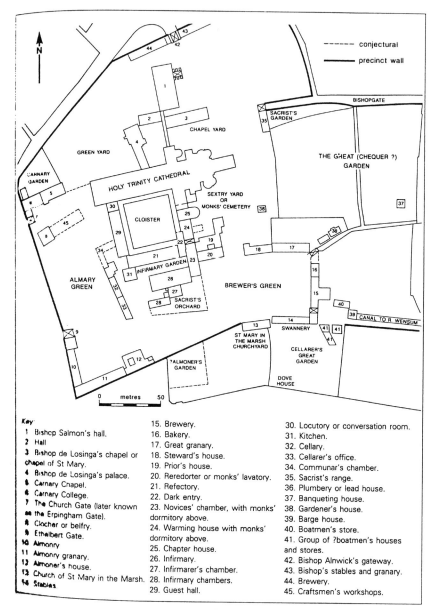

Key:
1 Bishop Salmon's hall.
2 Hall
3 Bishop de Losinga's chapel or chapel of St Mary.
4 Bishop de Losinga's palace.
5 Carnary Chapel.
6 Carnary College.
7 The Church Gate (later known as the Erpingham Gate).
8 Clocher or belfry.
9 Ethelbert Gate.
10 Almonry
11 Almonry granary.
12 Almoner's house.
13 Church of St Mary in the Marsh.
14 Stables

15. Brewery.
16. Bakery.
17. Great granary.
18. Steward's house.
19. Prior's house.
20. Reredorter or monks' lavatory.
21. Refectory.
22. Dark entry.
23. Novices' chamber, with monks' dormitory above.
24. Warming house with monks' dormitory above.
25. Chapter house.
26. Infirmary.
27. Infirmarer's chamber.
28. Infirmary chambers.
29. Guest hall.

30. Locutory or conversation room.
31. Kitchen.
32. Cellary.
33. Cellarer's office.
34. Communar's chamber.
35. Sacrist's range.
36. Plumbery or lead house.
37. Banqueting house.
38. Gardener's house.
39. Barge house.
40. Boatmen's store.
41. Group of ?boatmen's houses and stores.
42. Bishop Alnwick's gateway.
43. Bishop's stables and granary.
44. Brewery.
45. Craftsmen's workshops.

23.   Norwich: plan of precinct with bishop's palace on north side (Dodwell)

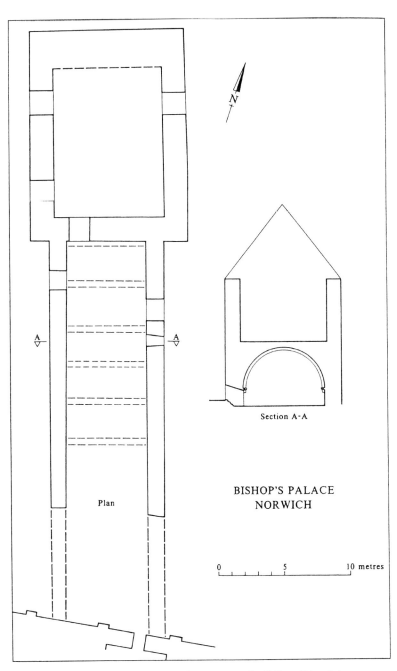

24. Norwich: plan and section of Losinga's building (Fernie)

gallery level (Whittingham, 1980; Atherton *et al.*, 1996, 110, 235). A range 6 m wide internally extends for 19.7 m at an angle of 80° to the nave with an enlargement of 8.2 by 12 m at its northern end (fig. 24). This perhaps constituted a tower in Continental fashion although the wall thickness of 1.8 m is certainly too thin to speak of a keep. The section against the church was covered on the ground floor by an original barrel vault, while the chamber or tower at the end had a later ribbed vault inserted.

Excavation has revealed beyond the north end a small two-storeyed building vaulted over the ground floor, called the 'small' hall although it looks like a chapel. Further south is a long building originally with apse, later squared off, regarded as the chapel. To the north again was the great aisled hall of Bishop Salmon (1299–1325), the last of the great episcopal aisled halls although sadly as at Canterbury only the porch survives.

Durham castle (p. 14) has already been mentioned. The domestic buildings are perhaps the best preserved so far as hall blocks go. Unfortunately the development is extremely complicated even with Martin Leyland (1994) to help us. There are two ranges on the north and west, presumably on the site of the 'palaces' of Prior Laurence (Thompson, 1994). The use of the word is very interesting applied to blocks in this way, rather as it is used in German sources. Leyland has discovered foundations of an eastern range going back to Bishop Walcher (1071–80), as he believes, being replaced by a northern range by Bishop Flambard (1099–1125). Apparently destruction by fire caused the more famous Bishop Puiset (1153–95) to carry out large-scale alterations including the fine decorated doorway and decorated arcades on the first floor (figs 106, 107).

The west range as it stands appears to be thirteenth century in date but in origin is much earlier, best seen in the undercroft under its north end. If its width required a single aisle this would be the nearest there is at Durham to the great aisled halls of the south or at Bishop Auckland in this diocese. The latter is so different from Puiset's work at Durham that it must raise doubts about its attribution to him. The chapel has been mentioned. There are other very interesting remains of later periods at the castle, which cannot be entered into here. The general effect of these two great ranges is to give more of a palace than castle feel to the buildings.

At Wolvesey, Winchester, extensive ruins adjoin the modern bishop's palace and have been investigated by Dr Martin Biddle over many years (Biddle, 1986). He has distinguished over 14 periods.

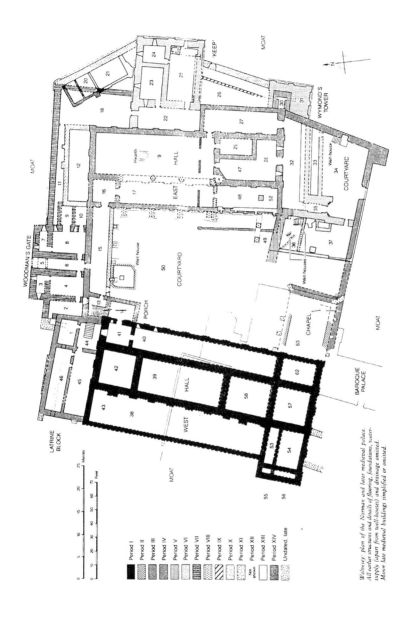

25. Wolvesey, Winchester: the bishop's palace. Plan after excavations. The west hall and protokeep are probably the earliest features. Note block design of halls with a single aisle in the later eastern hall (Biddle)

Wolvesey: plan of the Norman and later medieval palace. All earlier structures and details of flooring, foundations, water-supply (apart from well-houses) and drainage omitted. Minor late medieval buildings simplified or omitted.

WOODMAN'S GATE

MOAT

MOAT

LATRINE BLOCK

MOAT

WEST HALL

PORCH

COURTYARD

Well house

EAST HALL

Hearth

Well-house

COURTYARD

Well-house

CHAPEL

Well houses

MOAT

BAROQUE PALACE

'KEEP'

MOAT

WYMOND'S TOWER

N

Period I
Period II
Period III
Period IV
Period V
Period VI
Period VII
Period VIII
Period IX
Period X
Period XI
Period XII
Period XIII
Period XIV
Not shown
Undated, late

Metres

Feet

45

26.   Aerial view of Wolvesey from east with 'protokeep' in foreground. Note its pilasters, windows at ground level and stump of wall dividing off chamber at first-floor level (Cambridge Collection)

The two familiar long hall blocks on west and east are linked by a gateway on the north and a chapel on the south creating a kind of courtyard (figs 25, 26). On the east side is the 'protokeep' as I have called it (Thompson, 1995), two-storeyed, subdivided by pilasters on the outside, divided unequally on the inside with a smaller northern division again subdivided and probably originally with external steps on the south side. The downstairs windows are perhaps the most striking feature. A wall projected from its north-west corner but how it related to the original layout is not clear. Traces of pre-Conquest foundations have been found under the north gate. The west hall has a terrace on its outside and is assigned by Biddle to Bishop Giffard (1100–29). If it is related to the 'protokeep' it could presumably be even eleventh century. The east hall was a remarkably grand structure, a sort of hybrid, two-storeyed at the south end but an open hall with a single aisle arcade at the north, clearly earlier than the 'standard hall' of later in the century.

At Wolvesey we have the vexed question of trying to reconcile the reference of 1138 to 'domus quasi palatium cum turri fortissima' of the *Annales Wintoniae* (Luard, 1864, ii, 51) to what is visible today. The 'protokeep' does not qualify for the adjective 'fortissima', and although the east range might fit, bearing in mind that at Durham a single range is called a 'palatium', the events described are easier to explain if, as the 'Gesta Stephani' says, Henry of Blois had another house in town to which this refers (Potter, 1955, 84). There still remains much about the twelfth-century bishops of Winchester that we do not understand.

This concludes the long hall blocks of Continental style that formed see palaces but before turning to the thirteenth century there are two points to be made. The first is that the hall blocks were not confined to the see palaces, since two are known from the manors : Southwark and the archbishop of York's house at Otley, Yorkshire (fig. 27). In the latter case Jean le Patourel's excavation exposed the foundations of a two-storeyed chapel with apse vaulted on the ground floor that was converted into a long range with the chapel's east end squared off (Le Patourel, 1973). Southwark will be described under London.

Secondly three aisled halls at the sees have to be mentioned. The two in the far west, Hereford and Exeter, are remarkable for the use of wood in the arcades and arches (Blair, 1987). In the former case where much more survives (still inhabited by the bishop) John Blair has recently dated it to the later twelfth century, an imitation in wood of stonework (fig. 28). There was an earlier two-storeyed stone chapel at Hereford (fig. 42) but the form of the earliest palace is not known. At Exeter the building is even later, being attributed to Bishop Brewer (1224–44) (Chanter, 1932; Blaylock, 1990). Again the earliest form of palace is not known. At Old Sarum the foundations of the aisled hall revealed north of the cathedral must surely represent the first palace (fig. 29). They are of a stone building with central entry and apparently without services originally at one end; that is a pre-standard hall form. They have been attributed to Bishop Roger but in view of the Continental style of what he built in the royal castle (p. 24) one must wonder if it should be attributed to his predecessor, Osmund (1078–99), who has a distinctly native name, and perhaps was content with a native style hall.

Three palaces built over the same period of time, during the thirteenth century, hark back to the long blocks of the previous century, two-storeyed with vaulted ground floor but shorter: Wells, Worcester and Salisbury.

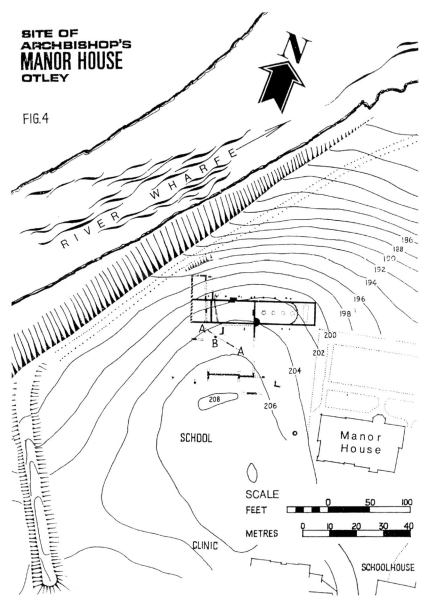

SITE OF ARCHBISHOP'S MANOR HOUSE OTLEY

FIG.4

27.   Otley, Yorkshire. A manor house of the archbishop of York, starting with an apsidal chapel, later converted into a long rectangular block (Le Patourel)

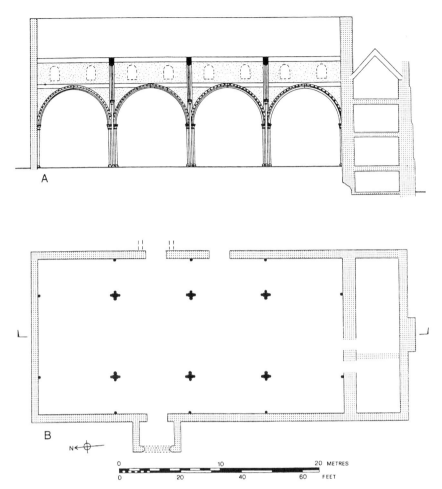

28.   Hereford: reconstructed section of the bishop's aisled hall with its wooden arcades (John Blair)

Wells with its moat, portcullis and resident bishop is perhaps the most rewarding see palace and has the advantage that it is open to the public during the summer (figs 30, 31). The main seat of the bishop of Bath and Wells from the thirteenth century was transferred south to Wells, Somerset, from Bath, where the site of the palace has been revealed by excavation (Chapman, Davenport and Holland, 1995), to the present site south of the cathedral at Wells during the episcopate of Jocelyn (1206–42). He built a two-storeyed rectangular building, vaulted over the ground floor, divided longitu-

OLD SARUM
CATHEDRAL AND ASSOCIATED BUILDINGS
Plan based on a survey by D. Montgomerie in Salisbury Museum. Dotted outlines
denote features attested by excavation, 1909-15. Features not outlined are assumed.

■ Late 11th century (Bishop Osmund)
▨ c.1110-25 (Bishop Roger)
▩ c.1142-1200 (Bishop Jocelyn and later)
▦ 13th century
☐ Uncertain
▨ Foundations of antecedent
    buildings
H Hearth   P Pit   W Well

29.   Old Sarum (Salisbury): cathedral and bishop's palace to the north,
probably 11th-century. Note primitive aisled hall with central entry and
absence of service doors (RCHME)

dinally into two parts, a narrow section about 5 m wide and a
broader part 8 m wide internally (fig. 32). The narrow part is subdivided by two cross walls at both levels, and the broad part has
two bays at its northern end separated off by a wall at both levels.
The five-bay compartment measures 22 by 8 m internally and clearly
should be designated a hall. There were not external steps but spiral
stairs at two corners. The narrow part is peculiar to Wells but surely
this is an updated hall block of familiar form. At its north-east
corner there is a projection for an oratory while at the south-west
corner there was originally a chapel of the same period, later rebuilt
by Burnell (1275–92) (fig. 33).
    What must have been the most impressive building on the site,
now a ruin, was added by Bishop Burnell at the same time as he
rebuilt the chapel. This was the great six-bay hall, the west bay
containing the pantry and buttery with passage to external kitchen.

30.   Wells, Somerset: aerial view of bishop's palace and beyond it the cathedral. Note large enclosing moat, Jocelyn's two-storeyed hall (roofed), chapel and remains of Burnell's late 13th-century aisled hall (Cambridge Collection)

Its porch on the north side has corner turrets like the main building. It is substantially later than the aisled halls at Lincoln and Canterbury but appreciably earlier than that at Norwich. It is sad that these great halls at the see palaces are so fragmentary and it is necessary to turn to the bishop of Durham's hall at Bishop Auckland to appreciate what one looked like (figs 34, 35). The defensive features and gateway are later, as are the group of buildings to the north built by Bishop Bekyngton (1443–65). These were linked by a cloister in the later middle ages.

At Worcester the deanery, formerly the bishop's palace, has some evidence in parallel walls of an early range, but the main construction was undertaken by Bishop Giffard (1268–1302) (*VCH, Worcs*, iv, 406–8). The hall of four bays has a vaulted ground floor. Later alterations have made it a confusing plan.

Salisbury has been discussed to some extent already (p. 25). We are concerned with Bishop Poore's hall after the move down to its

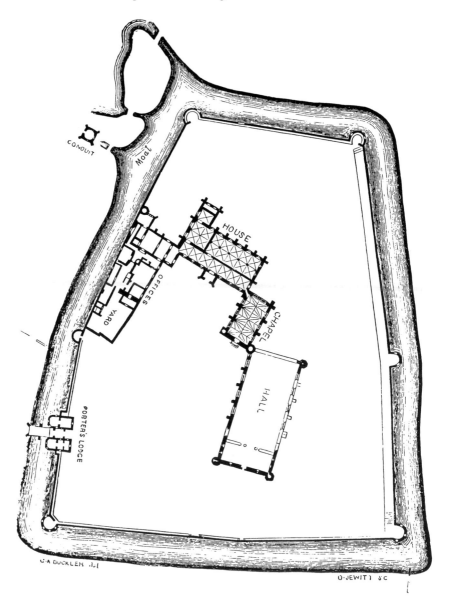

GENERAL PLAN.

31. Wells: plan of palace (Parker)

Entrance Hall.

The work of Bishop Jocelyne, A.D. 1205–1244.

Servants' Hall.

32. Wells: the divided vaulted undercroft of Jocelyn's hall of early 13th century (Parker)

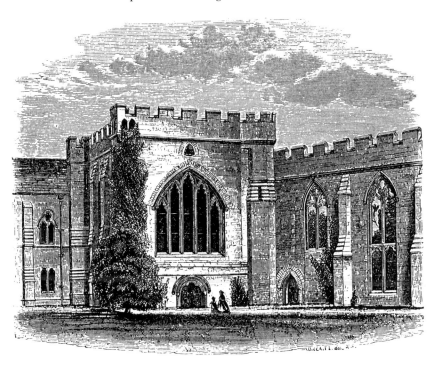

West end of the Chapel, with part of Bishop Jocelyne's House and Bishop Burnell's Hall.

33.   Wells: west door of chapel with Jocelyn's hall on left and Burnell's on right (Parker)

modern site within the city. The Royal Commission that studied the building in detail published a coloured dated plan.[1] I have been influenced by contemporary work at Wells and particularly Jocelyn's hall. We would expect the original hall at Salisbury to be on the first floor and this I suggest is what the Commission calls the 'solar', while the chapel would have to be at right-angles to be oriented. The aisled hall at the east end can only have been rebuilt in the fifteenth century after a fire or disaster, for aisled halls were not being built at that date. The original aisled hall was perhaps late thirteenth century following a similar linear development to Wells and in the same position (figs 36, 37).

Chichester see palace is very confusing although evidently a medieval building (*VCH, Sussex*, iii, 147–53). A great square kitchen on the east side, possibly twelfth century, and the chapel with one bay two-storeyed to the north of it are the most striking features. One

Drawn by R. W.Billings.   *Engraved by G. B. Smith.*

34.   Bishop Auckland, County Durham: a 19th-century view of the
aisled hall of c.1200 converted at the Restoration into a chapel. The
service doors were behind the reredos

has a distinct feeling that a great hall, since pulled down, existed
between the two wings.

   The monastic partner of Lichfield, Coventry, gave its name to the
see. The medieval cathedral of Coventry was St Mary's abbey, of

35.   Bishop Auckland: view of the arcade in the converted hall
(Rollason)

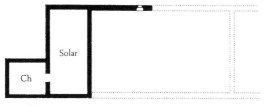

First Floor

Ground Floor
a. c.1225

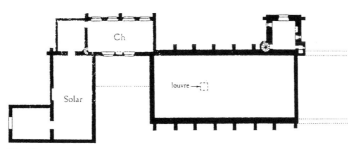

First Floor

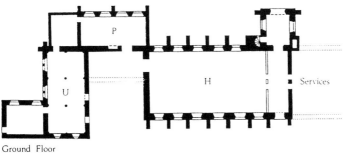

Ground Floor
b. c.1470

36.   Salisbury: RCHME's change from 1225 to c.1470. It is suggested that the 'solar' of 1225 was the original hall (cf. Wells) and that a late 13th-century hall was reconstructed in the 15th century as shown by the Commission

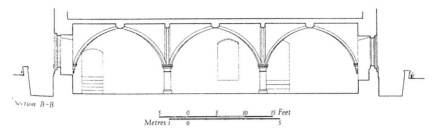

Section B-B

5   0   5   10   15 Feet

Metres 1   0   5

37. Salisbury: the undercroft of the original hall ('solar') of Bishop Poore (RCHME)

which few traces now remain. The site of the see palace on land granted in 1224–5 is just east of the modern cathedral of St Michael (Lilley, 1994). Earlier a palace may also have existed at Chester at the church of St John. It is, however, the medieval palace at Lichfield that concerns us.

The see palace at Lichfield, Staffordshire, has completely vanished but it is known from detailed drawings made before demolition in 1685 (Tringham, 1993; *VCH, Staffs*, xiv, 63). It was erected by Bishop Walter de Langton (1296–1321) in a surprising place to the north east of the church. Whether it had been in a different position before, it is impossible to say (fig. 38). The construction of the palace formed an integral part of the massive fortification of the close wall against which it was built. Towers projecting from the wall extended backwards to form chambers at either end of the hall, one of them creating an apse for the chapel. The hall, which measured some 30 m by 17 m (100 × 56 ft), was raised over a vaulted undercroft and entered by external steps. It can hardly have had aisle arcades over an undercroft but its roof span must have required division : can it have had a double gable and spinal arcade like the almost exactly contemporary hall of Philipe le Bel in the palais royal in Paris? The kitchen at the south end was reached by steps. Walter de Langton had been involved with Edward I's Welsh wars which were commemorated in paintings in the palace. It is unfortunate that this very interesting building does not survive.

Finally we come to the see palaces in the four Welsh dioceses. Llandaff has been treated as a castle (p. 25). At St Asaph, the poorest see, no palace is known before the eighteenth century, although a T-shaped farmhouse known as Esgobty down a lane to the south west of the cathedral may have served the bishop in at least the sixteenth century.[2] At Bangor the town hall is the former bishop's palace, a part of which is a timber-framed building of the early sixteenth century.[3]

In contrast St Davids bishop's palace is one of the most impressive in Britain. The setting within a deep valley behind the cathedral is quite extraordinarily evocative (Frontispiece). The ruins, which stand largely to full height, are open to the public. St Davids in medieval times had become the premier see in Wales and was the bishopric to which Giraldus Cambrensis tried so hard to secure election without success. Although the palace will always be associated with the name of Bishop Henry of Gower (1328–47), a Welshman who had been Chancellor of Oxford University, the buildings have a decidedly Welsh character about them (Williams, 1981).

The palace consists of a square courtyard entered by a fourteenth-century gateway on the north side (fig. 39). Low foundations on the west side possibly belong to a twelfth-century arrangement but are just as likely to be the remains of service buildings (fig. 40) (Radford, 1955).[4] Immediately inside the gate on the left is a two-storeyed fourteenth-century chapel serving the east range, which is at first-floor level on continuous transverse vaults over the ground floor, forming separate rooms entered from the courtyard. Both ranges east and south are raised in similar fashion. I know of no parallel in England. The east range is 7 m wide and the south range 10 m wide internally. Seemingly the east range is late thirteenth century in date, although recently attributed to an early phase of Henry Gower's work, while the south range is Henry of Gower by tradition, for there is no documentary evidence. It is a classic case of an enlargement of accommodation by the addition of a larger hall, the earlier smaller one no doubt reverting to private quarters for the bishop. The two were so placed that their lower ends adjoined and could be served by a new kitchen at this point. Both ranges were partitioned at the upper end to provide chamber accommodation for the bishop. The new range made use of an earlier chapel apparently related to the earliest buildings (fig. 39). Henry's hall had a most elaborate porch, with niches for statuary, covering the steps up to the hall. This hall has a rose window in its eastern gable.

The palace of St Davids illustrates how different was the course of hall development in Wales from England; not entirely different, for the creation of lower and higher ends is a common feature. At a time when one might have expected in England the use of ground floor and probably aisled halls, in Wales they are still uncompromisingly

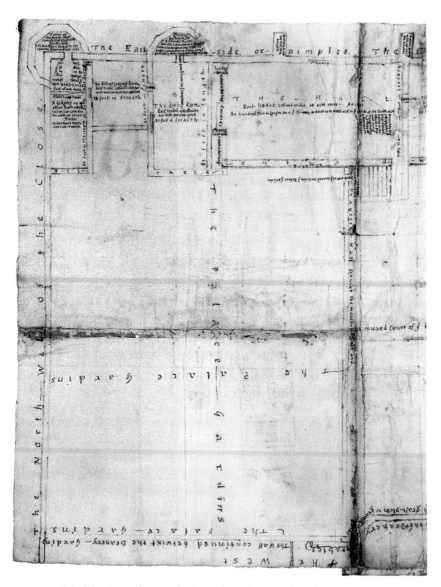

38.   Lichfield: plan of 1685 before demolition of Bishop Langton's palace built c.1300. Note how the towers on the strongly fortified close wall were used castle-fashion

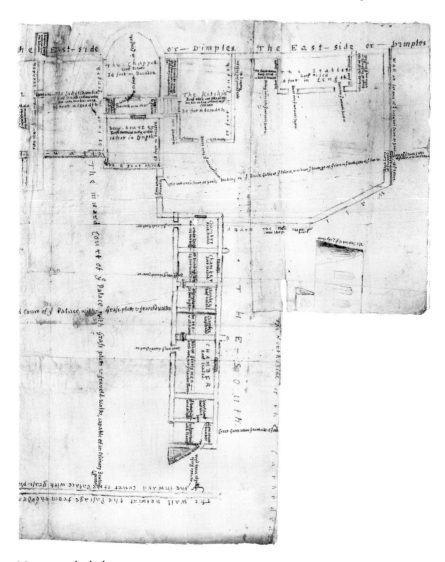

38.   *concluded*

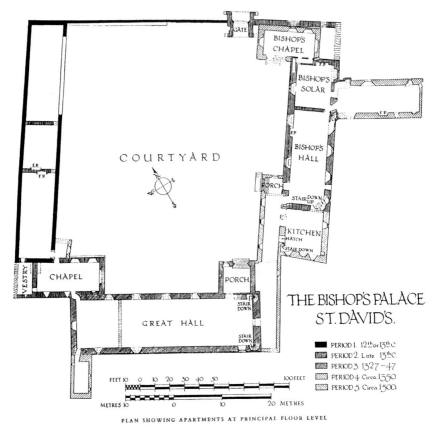

39.   St Davids, Pembrokeshire: plan of the bishop's palace at first-floor level. Note the earlier small hall, superseded by Henry of Gower's 14th-century larger hall, both set over transverse vaults (Radford)

raised to first floor level. Chambers were created by partition not by transverse wings. These are still in many respects Continental hall blocks not English barn-style halls. The contrast is clear when you have English intrusions into Wales by Edward I, or Edward II at Caerphilly in Glamorgan.

There remains one highly distinctive feature of the St Davids palace, a sort of hallmark of Henry of Gower, that so enhances the appearance of his buildings (fig. 41). At St Davids it is used not only on his new work but applied to the older work also to give uniformity. It is also used at the bishop's house at Lamphey, Pembrokeshire and very dramatically at Swansea castle, Glamorgan. The wall walk

Episcopal Palace, at S.ʰDavids Pembrokeshire.

40.   St Davids bishop's palace, a 19th-century view. Note the open arcades below the parapet and the ogee-headed doorway with niches above leading to Henry of Gower's hall. Cf. the air photo in Frontispiece

was raised on an arcade in such a way that the slope of the roof passed down between the arches (figs 40, 41) and the rainwater could be thrown off directly from a deep eave. However, I do not believe that this was the main intention. It had no defensive function for it weakened the whole superstructure which would have collapsed under bombardment. The intention was surely entirely decorative, which is certainly its effect. The inspiration may have come from seeing machicolation perhaps abroad and either misunderstanding it or quite intentionally using it as a motif. As the roof slope prevented access, and in any case there was no overhang or shelter, it could not possibly have had any defensive value. Once seen at St Davids or Swansea it will not be easily forgotten for it transforms the building to which it is applied.

PARAPET OF THE CHAPEL.

CHIMNEY ON THE EAST SIDE OF THE
QUADRANGLE.

MOULDING OF THE PRINCIPAL ENTRANCE FROM
THE QUADRANGLE.

DETAILS OF THE PALACE

41.   St Davids: detail from the palace showing especially the arcading
below the parapet associated with Henry of Gower

iv   Two-storeyed chapels

The conversion of two of the finest bishops' halls at Bishop Auckland and Mayfield after the middle ages into chapels has given us a very misleading idea of medieval bishops' chapels. Both the halls have converted into very impressive chapels but they are on the ground floor whereas chapels in bishops' houses with very rare exceptions were two-storeyed with a crypt or undercroft that was quite serviceable for worship. They were normally but not always vaulted.

As bishop's houses, especially on the manors and in London, are normally indistinguishable from those of the laity at the same social level, this distinction of the form of chapel is of especial interest, marking out a house as episcopal. It is not unknown with royalty: the Sainte Chapelle in Paris comes to mind. Incidentally, this chapel is no doubt important for the influence of its tracery and detail, as the art historians tell us, but two-storeyed chapels had a long history before this. In origin they may have arisen so that the first floor coincided with the main floor of an adjoining range and while this may be true on the Continent a curious fact is that the early ones in this country seem to have been free-standing at least initially: Hereford, Durham and Otley.

The other point that must arise is how were they intended to be used? Was the ground floor for laity and the first floor for the use of the bishop and ecclesiastics? Very elaborate examples look as if they were intended for relics and I have suggested, half seriously, that at Durham St Cuthbert was placed there temporarily while the cathedral was being built (Thompson, 1994). There is probably no definitive answer.

It might be helpful to make a list of these episcopal two-storeyed chapels, arranged roughly chronologically for they cover the whole of the middle ages, not an exhaustive list but including examples known from excavations or only in written sources. References will be found in the Working List, unless otherwise stated.

Canterbury. By west range of cloister, demolished
Hereford (fig. 42)
Durham (fig. 6, p. 16)
Otley, Yorkshire (fig. 27). Excavated by Mrs Le Patourel
Wolvesey, Winchester
Sherborne castle, Dorset (fig. 57)
Old Sarum castle (fig. 11)
York. All that survives of the palace

42.   Hereford: plan and elevation of the 11th-century bishop's chapel in 1738 before destruction (Society of Antiquaries)

Lambeth Palace. Fine undercroft but chapel above restored after bombing (fig. 43)

Southwark. Known from excavation (Carlin, 1985)

Chichester. One bay only

St Davids. Two chapels

Lichfield. Known from 1685 survey

Holborn, Ely house. All that survives of bishop of Ely's house, now St Etheldreda's Roman catholic church. Floor supported on wooden posts (figs 44, 45)

Charing, Kent

Croydon, Surrey (fig. 94)

Saltwood castle, Kent. Archbishop Courtenay's work

Knole, Kent

York Place, Whitehall. Excavation (Thurley, 1991)

v   Summary

There was apparently no see palace at Carlisle and St Asaph. The main buildings have disappeared at London, York (except the chapel),

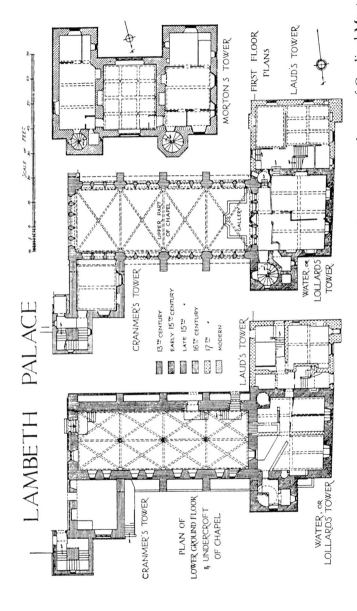

LAMBETH PALACE

CRANMER'S TOWER

PLAN OF
LOWER GROUND FLOOR
& UNDERCROFT
OF CHAPEL

WATER, OR
LOLLARDS' TOWER

CRANMER'S TOWER

13ᵀᴴ CENTURY
EARLY 15ᵀᴴ CENTURY
LATE 15ᵀᴴ "
16ᵀᴴ CENTURY "
17ᵀᴴ "
MODERN

UPPER PART
OF CHAPEL

GALLERY

WATER OR
LOLLARDS
TOWER

MORTON'S TOWER

SCALE OF FEET

FIRST FLOOR
PLANS

LAUD'S TOWER

LAUD'S TOWER

43. Lambeth Palace: the chapel of c.1200 at both levels and the late 15th-century gatehouse of Cardinal Morton (RCHME)

Ely House, London . Pl.1.

44. London, Ely House, Holborn: an 18th-century view of the bishop's chapel of c.1300 with cloister and hall beyond

Lichfield, Bath and Coventry. Excavation has located the last two and Lichfield is known from a seventeenth-century survey. At Ely the main palace is lost but its brick flanking wings survive. Only at Hereford, Wells and Chichester does the modern bishop occupy the medieval see palace: at Lambeth, Fulham, Bishop Auckland and Bishopthorpe he still lives in a medieval house, and at Rose castle and Hartlebury castle in medieval manor castles.

At Durham the see palace was a castle throughout the middle ages; at Lincoln and Old Sarum the royal castle was temporarily occupied by the bishop. At Llandaff the see palace was a castle, if one can apply this term, from the thirteenth to fifteenth centuries.

The normal arrangement for the Norman bishops clearly was to erect a two-storey hall block (*Saalbau*) as close as they could make it to the Continental form, with a chamber formed by a partition wall on the first floor. A two-storeyed chapel might be attached to it or built freestanding. Old Sarum had an aisled hall from the beginning and the position is not clear in a number of other sees. A shorter first-floor hall seems not uncommon in the thirteenth cen-

View in the Undercroft of the chapel of Ely palace, Holborn.

Drawn 1776. Engrav'd & Pub.d Jan.1.1786. by J. Carter Wod S. West.

45. Ely House, Holborn: a view in 1776 of the wooden posts in the underchapel supporting the floor of the main chapel above (Carter)

tury but gradually a large aisled hall becomes usual, leaving the older hall as a private quarter for the bishop. In Wales (and Scotland) this did not happen, perhaps for security reasons, and the old first-floor hall ruled supreme. The later courtyard development that we shall see on the manors hardly took place in the close.

Notes

1.   RCHME (1993), *Salisbury: Houses of the Close*, 53–83.
2.   Listed building. Information from RCAHMW.
3.   RCAHMW, *Carn.* ii, 9–10, fig. 19.
4.   W. Evans attributes the early hall to initial Henry Gower but his Cadw plan, 1991, shows a thirteenth-century wall at its south end. He makes other emendations to dating.

The bishops had several reasons for visiting London. Many of them acted as ministers to the Crown, varying from the chief minister, 'Viceroy', like Bishop Roger of Salisbury (1101–39), to humbler functions and in the later middle ages a bishopric was normally earned by long and efficient service to the Crown. They had also to attend Court or from the thirteenth-century Parliament. They also had their own business which could be political, legal or simply social. A London 'inn' or *hospicium*, a sort of *pied à terre*, became essential for a bishop from the thirteenth century. Schofield (1995, 34) found 20 bishops and 22 abbots as having London houses: only one Welsh bishop, of St Asaph, apparently never had one. Almost all our information on the situation of these inns comes from John Stow's *Survey of London* (the third edition of 1633 is used in this book) which tells us where houses had been, since by that time most bishops had been forced to give them up, covetous eyes having been cast on such valuable sites at the Reformation.

The earliest of the inns was at Southwark, Winchester House. Its construction was formerly attributed to Giffard (1100–29) but the discovery of a document has caused a revision and it is now attributed to Henry of Blois. He is reported to have said that on account of 'the inconveniences caused to him and his predecessors he obtained land from Ongar the Rich and the monks of Bermondsey, (Schofield, 1995). It is on the right or south bank of the Thames on the river front, very near to what is now Southwark cathedral. By the end of the twelfth century the bishop of Rochester and archbishop of Canterbury had established themselves further upstream on the same side of the river. The sees south of the Thames had their houses on the south side of the river except Chichester which later acquired a site in Chancery Lane as a gift from Henry III; this partly survives in Lincolns Inn (*ibid.*, no. 47).

On the left bank the earliest house was of about the same date, erected by Bishop Robert de Cheney of Lincoln (1148–66). Presumably to avoid the jurisdiction of the bishop of London most of the bishops' houses were to the west of the City wall and particularly along the river frontage between London and Westminster. The advantage of the river frontage was for travel, the bishop maintaining his own barge to move up and down stream in the most comfortable form of travel. Details of some of the houses, as described by Stow, will be found in the Working List at the end of the book while dates of foundation are given by Schofield (1995, 35): Bath and Wells 1231–8, Durham 1237, Norwich 1237, Carlisle 1238, York 1240–5. None of these survive.

A very interesting late foundation was that by the bishop of Durham at Bridgecourt in Battersea with a licence of 1474 to crenellate with towers and impark,[1] a sort of *rus in urbe*! Wolsey's work was the climax of this at Whitehall and Bridewell (acquired by the king afterwards) and at the bishop of Durham's Bridgecourt (Thurley, 1991, 77). Wolsey was archbishop of York from 1514, bishop of Durham 1523 and at the end bishop of Winchester from 1529.

The recent publication of Wyngaerde's drawings of London in c. 1544 (Colvin and Foster, 1996) had an interesting view of the river frontage on the left bank showing the inn of the bishop of Bath and Wells and in the background the hall and two-storeyed chapel of the bishop of Ely. The gardens along the river frontage indicate how very agreeable some of these London houses must have been. The proximity of the inns on land or across the river by boat must have encouraged an active social life: no wonder the length of the periods of stay of the bishops in London tended to increase!

i   Right bank

Of all the London houses only at two, Lambeth, still in use, and the Winchester House fragments at Southwark, are there sufficient remains to make a real description possible.

We are extremely fortunate that the remains at Southwark have been recently studied making use of the Winchester Pipe Rolls (Carlin, 1985). What we see today is merely a fragment of a large establishment, a house with two courtyards and a river frontage, a large garden and a private dock on the east side. The bishop of Rochester had his later inn immediately behind Winchester house. The Winchester Pipe Rolls begin in 1208 but are fairly laconic until the second half of the century as one can see by comparing the published years of 1209 and 1210 with their slim volumes to the thick volume of 1301–2. A new hall has been identified as referring to the existing fragment. This consists of a tall gable containing the well-known rose window and below the three service doorways, a frag-

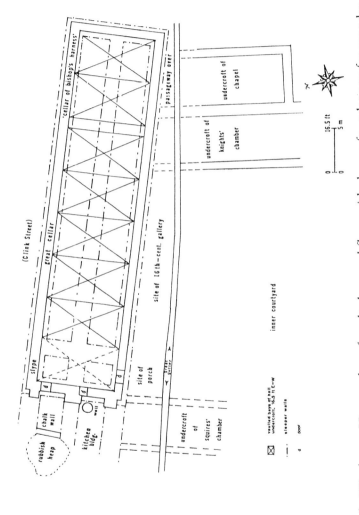

46. Southwark, Winchester House: plan of vaulted ground floor with sleeper foundations for wooden uprights. Note wall separating chamber from hall in the floor above (Carlin)

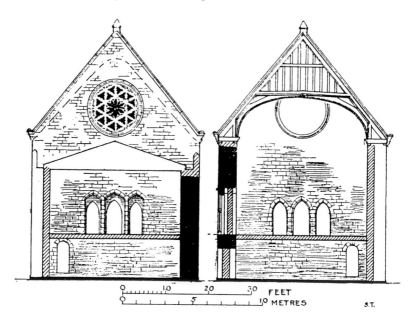

47. Southwark, Winchester House: the gable wall with the rose window over the service doors at lower end of hall (S. Toy)

ment of south wall with a doorway, all set in a long narrow range 8.7 m wide internally, with a basement or undercroft vaulted its full length with spinal piers to support the vault (figs 46, 47). There was an internal division evidently to form the chamber at first-floor level. This hall block (*Saalbau*), for that is what it is, was built along the river frontage. As it is called the new hall the original hall of Henry of Blois had already been superseded, and perhaps lay south of the chapel and parallel, where the bishop's chamber is marked. This substitution would allow use of the same chapel. The contrast with the style of hall just upstream at Lambeth Palace, probably originally aisled and only a few decades later, is remarkable. I would be surprised if the Southwark hall is much later than 1190. With Otley it is the only hall block known outside the see palaces.

One of the advantages of having a house on the right bank was that there was almost unlimited space: the archbishop of Canterbury had his deer park at Lambeth, so did the bishop of Durham later further upstream at Battersea. It is noticeable both at Southwark and at Lambeth that the living accommodation was right on the water (tidal) edge. This was convenient for travel by boat although the bishop of Winchester had the alternative of London bridge close by.

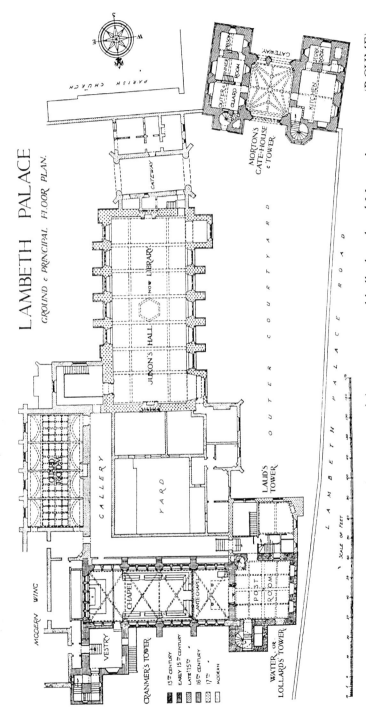

LAMBETH PALACE

GROUND & PRINCIPAL FLOOR PLAN.

MODERN WING

VESTRY

CRANMER'S TOWER

13TH CENTURY
EARLY 15TH CENTURY
LATE 15TH
16TH CENTURY
17TH
MODERN

GUARD ROOM

GALLERY

YARD

CHAPEL

ANTE-CHAPEL

POST ROOM

WATER, OR LOLLARDS TOWER

LAUD'S TOWER

JUXON'S HALL

NOW LIBRARY

GATEWAY

PARISH CHURCH

OUTER COURTYARD

OUTER INNER GUARD ROOM

GATEWAY

KITCHEN

STORE ROOM

MORTON'S GATE-HOUSE & TOWER

L A M B E T H   P A L A C E   R O A D

SCALE OF FEET

48. Lambeth Palace: plan showing the position of the reconstructed hall, chapel and Morton's gateway (RCHME)

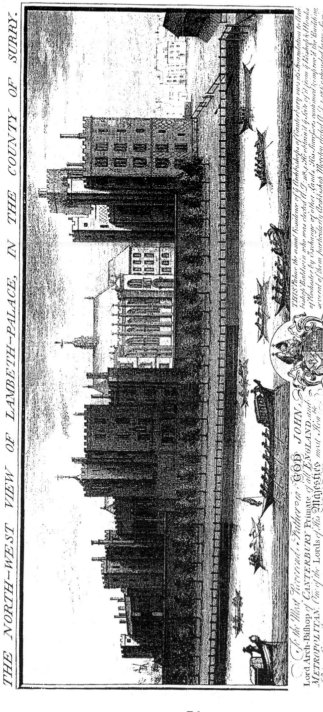

49. Lambeth Palace: view from the river in 1737 by the Buck brothers. Morton's gatehouse on the right (church tower behind), Juxom's restored hall with the Lollard's tower on the left

Although the archbishop of Canterbury still lives in Lambeth Palace the buildings have had a rough time, particularly during the Civil War when the hall was destroyed and was entirely rebuilt at the Restoration by Archbishop Juxon (1660–5) (figs 48, 49). He gave the hall a hammer beam roof and central hearth, so it is a remarkable case of 'survival revival'. If it corresponds in the original dimensions then the medieval hall measured 27 by 12 m internally with seven bays and screens, and a porch at the south end. At present the chapel on the north is linked to the hall by a kind of cloister. The chapel is two-storeyed with a very fine vaulted ground floor of four bays, c. 1200. At its west end is a square tower known as Lollard's or Water tower which formerly projected into the Thames. An annex known as Laud's tower, after the seventeenth-century archbishop, projects from this. The other significant medieval building is what is known as the guardroom, a fourteenth-century building with a fine timber roof, to the east.[2]

The entry from the south (near Lambeth Bridge) passes through a massive brick gateway consisting of two rectangular towers of unequal size flanking a vaulted gate passage with a separate pedestrian archway. The greater width of the western tower than the eastern one gives a curiously lop-sided effect outside. Archbishop Morton (1486–1500) constructed this building of brick with stone dressings, which is an example of the overbearing gateways that will be more fully discussed in Chapter 6.

ii   Left bank

On this side of the Thames survival is limited to the late thirteenth-century chapel of St Etheldreda at Holborn belonging to the inn of the bishops of Ely, although records and a survey with drawings provide much information about the rest of the inn (Schofield, 1995, no. 106; Aston, 1967, 271–5) (figs 50, 51). Wolsey's extensive works at York Place have been investigated (Thurley, 1991). Records have again provided much information on the very conspicuous inn of the bishop of Bath and Wells (Kingsford, 1922; Schofield, 1995, no. 15): a view by Hollar in 1646 when it was in later ownership gives us a glimpse of how such a medieval inn might have looked in the bishops' time (fig. 52).

The culmination of bishops' riverside residences was reached, albeit abruptly cut short, under Cardinal Wolsey who as archbishop

Published 26. Oct. 1784. by S Hooper.   Dent Sculp

50.   Ely House, Holborn: view from Holborn in 1786 of the late 13th-century hall

of York set about improving York Place (Thurley, 1991). It may be remarked that as Wolsey did not visit York until his fall from grace, hitherto being London-based he is the extreme example of the absentee bishop of the period. At York Place Thurley has worked out the sequence which subsequently became part of Henry VIII's Whitehall. It had been in use for 200 years by archbishops of York so that the main buildings such as the hall already existed on the site. Wolsey's first alterations were to create a new great chamber on the opposite side of the cloister building linked by a raised gallery with the hall. His next addition was a long gallery along the riverside, and only when he had acquired more land did he undertake full reconstruction of the hall and virtually the whole house to conform more to his own views (fig. 53). The long gallery along the river front certainly suggests a Renaissance idea (*ibid.*, fig. 5).

Bridewell palace, further downstream towards the City, where Wolsey had started, became a royal palace in 1515 (*ibid.*, 80ff). There has been much recent work on the site.

Leaving the river for Holborn the later records give a good idea of the bishop of Ely's house as it survived 200 years after it had passed

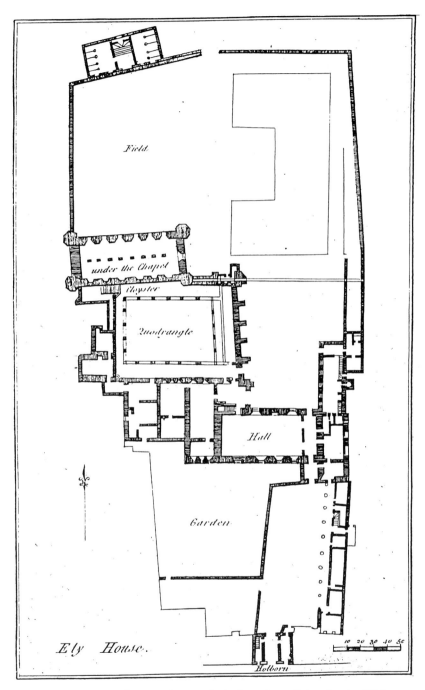

51.   Ely House, Holborn: plan made before demolition in the 18th
century. Cf. figs. 44, 45 and 50

Aula Domus Arrundeliana Londini.   Septentrionem versus.

52.   Arundel House, Strand, London: formerly Bath Inn of the bishops of Bath and Wells. Although buildings on left and right are post-medieval the hall range must date from late medieval times

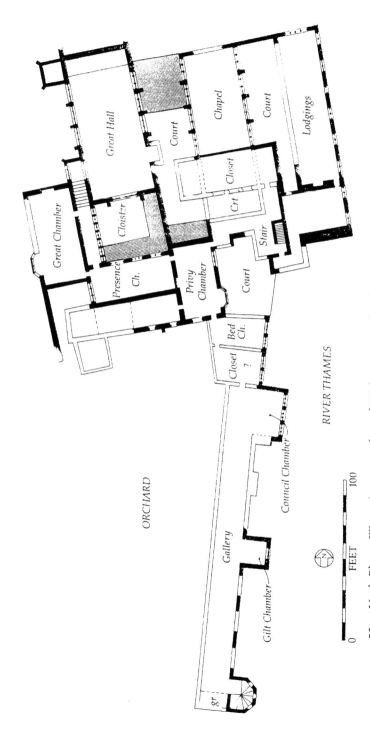

ORCHARD

Great Chamber

Presence Ch.

Cloister

Great Hall

Court

Privy Chamber

Court

Court

Closet

Chapel

Crt

Court

Stair

Lodgings

Closet

Bed Ch.

?

Council Chamber

Gallery

Gilt Chamber

8r

RIVER THAMES

N

FEET

0   100

53. York Place, Westminster: a plan of Wolsey's completed reconstruction in 1529 (Thurley)

out of episcopal hands (figs 50, 51). Entering from Holborn on the south side one approached the hall at its east end; the screens passage was of the usual kind with kitchen on the right. The chamber wing at the west end fronted on its north side with a cloister. In the later middle ages cloisters for walking without attached ranges were increasingly popular in secular architecture. The cloisters at New College, Oxford, or Winchester College are good surviving examples. They could be used as a link between buildings as at Wells although to judge by the drawings at Ely House there had been ranges of buildings on the alleys. The chapel and hall on opposite sides of the cloister have a monastic feel which may well have been intended.

The bishop's chapel, now St Etheldreda's church serving a Roman Catholic community, is accessible, more so than most episcopal chapels. It is two-storeyed but not vaulted over the ground floor which has a central row of posts on stone bases supporting the wooden floor of the main church above (fig. 45). The property was brought to the see by John of Kirkby, bishop 1286–90, at which time the hall was built with the chapel being erected by his successor, William of Louth (1290–8).

Summary

If the chapter can be summarised, 20 of the 21 Welsh and English sees had acquired an inn in London by gift or purchase from the twelfth but mainly thirteenth centuries. They were situated principally between London and Westminster to a great extent along the riverside with three or four on the right bank. All the bishops visited London several times a year with visits probably becoming longer as the middle ages advanced. Often furnished with fine gardens they did not differ greatly from houses of the secular laity of the same social status. Southwark still used the Continental-style hall block but so far as we can tell the barn-style hall was normal in other houses. The bishops were usually forced out at the Reformation, except of course at Lambeth, the only true survivor.

Notes

1. *Calendar of Charter Rolls*, 1474, p. 242.

2. RCHME, *London*, ii, 79–86. A survey of 1647 at Lambeth Palace Library, *Comm, xiia/23/62*, describes 'a foure square cloyster reaching from the chappell to the halle' with over it 'the greate library of the Arch Bishopricke', the whole being covered with lead. This is recalled in the present open courtyard with library on three sides.

5   *Castles on the manors*

We have seen that there was something anomalous, if not improper, about a bishop constructing his see palace in the form of a castle, so always (except at Llandaff, where there were special circumstances) it was a royal castle that the bishop took over, temporarily except at Durham. On his manors the bishop found himself in quite a different position: most of the inhibitions that existed in the precinct of the cathedral no longer obtained. There might be objections in canon law to a bishop building or at all events holding a castle, as Bishop Roger found out at the end of his life, but in the real world a bishop on his manor was not in a very different position from a lay lord (Kealey, 1972, 95).

There is no special evidence that bishops had a weakness for castle-building in the eleventh century. It is not something we associate with Odo, for example. Bishop Gundulph of Rochester (1077–1108) is said to have been involved with the construction of the White Tower for the king at the Tower of London (*HKW*, i, 29). The tower at the cathedral itself (p. 14) and the one at West Malling are attributed to him. It is difficult to think of any other bishops with similar claims.

It is possible that in the eleventh century some residual doubts existed about whether the bishop enjoyed full rights, as opposed to the chapter or convent, over his manors (p. 3). The idea of creating or promoting a borough that is intimately connected with castle construction is related since it affected the potential value of the manor. In the thirteenth century the desire to create or promote a borough is evident but without the previous need to build a castle to promote the action (Beresford, 1959). About a quarter of the boroughs founded in medieval times recorded by Beresford and Finberg (1973) had ecclesiastical founders of one kind or another, 143 out of 609 (Table 3) and mostly after 1100 (Table 4).

The first half of the twelfth century was a particularly propitious time for castle founding as indeed it was for the founding of monasteries. Henry I, a great castle builder himself both in England and Normandy, seems to have taken a very relaxed attitude to others doing the same thing. After his death castle-building reached something of a climax. Three bishops, perhaps four, were particularly involved in this activity according to the chroniclers, and as these were very remarkable men they deserve individual attention (cf. Potter, 1955).

i   Bishop Roger of Salisbury (1101–39)

It is fortunate that this bishop has been the subject of a valuable biography by Kealey (1972) where all the references bearing on his life will be found. Born in about 1065 he was a priest in Avranches when Henry I selected him to fill the see at Salisbury. He enjoyed an exceptionally long episcopacy of 38 years and during the absences of the king was virtually the ruler, the 'Viceroy', in this country. He combined his ecclesiastical office with the secular one of Chancellor, so his resources and authority were very great. He was a man of considerable innovative and administrative ability, being credited with the creation of the Exchequer which was an immediate success (Kealey, 1972, 26). The four castles that he built or enlarged may be considered.

In south Wales the English or rather Normans were seeking to establish themselves. After the death of Hywel ab Gronw in 1106, land was granted to the bishop of Salisbury (Fox and Radford, 1935) at Kidwelly in Dyfed. A castle of semi-circular form was laid out on the banks of the river Gwendraeth with an attached borough to the south; later extended to the north (figs 54, 55). The later stone gateway on the borough earthwork survives although the town has since departed to the other side of the river. The stone walls and towers on top of the castle earthworks belong to the thirteenth century and later, erected long after bishops had anything to do with the place. It is a remarkable survival and shows fairly closely what the bishop did in 1106–15. More important from our point of view is that the experience in Wales no doubt caused Bishop Roger to try his hand at doing the same thing in his diocese in England.

The castle at Devizes, Wiltshire, attracted great admiration from contemporaries : 'the most splendid castle in Europe' according to Henry of Huntingdon (quoted by Kealey, 1972, 89). There is little doubt that he was impressed as much by the borough as by the castle itself, which were not always clearly distinguished from each other. The remains indicate (Stone, 1920) that it started with a motte and bailey (fig. 56). This may have been earlier than Bishop

54.   Kidwelly, Carmarthenshire: an aerial view from north showing the castle and old borough with gateway, stone replacement of Bishop Roger of Salisbury's original castle and borough (Cambridge Collection)

Roger. He was responsible for building the great rectangular keep with its unequal division within this enclosure, and no doubt for a lot more masonry structures. It is, however, the eastward extension

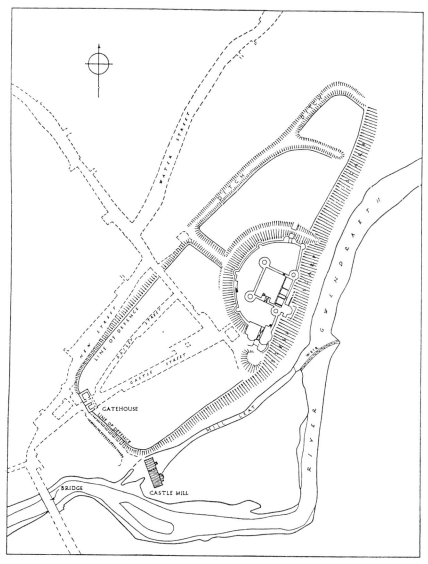

55.   Kidwelly: plan of castle and old borough (Fox and Radford, *Arch.*, 83)

creating a borough recorded in a charter of 1135–9 (*EMB*, 178) that was his main contribution. There are in fact two extensions from the castle, each with a church, the second perhaps being later than Roger. The castle, parks and borough were acquired by the Crown in 1157 (*ibid.*).

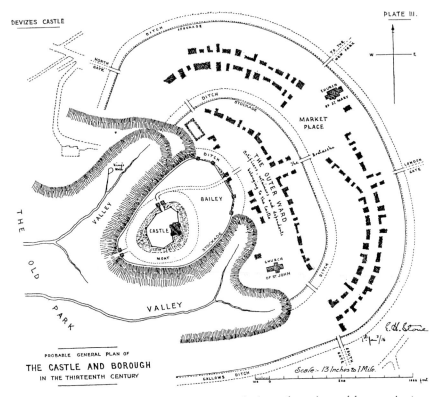

56.   Devizes: E. H. Stone's reconstructed plan of castle and boroughs in the 13th century. Note the two churches in the earlier and later stages. Bishop Roger may have been responsible for both

At Malmesbury, Wiltshire, we know from the *Historia Novella* (Potter, 1955) that the bishop began a castle in the pre-Conquest borough using stone fallen from the church (*EMB*, 179). Nothing survives of this castle. The intention no doubt was to promote the existing borough.

This leaves Sherborne or more strictly Castleton, Dorset.[1] There is reference to a borough as late as 1538 (*EMB*) but whether the bishop intended one or where it was is not clear. There seems to be no junction with the curtain wall indicating an outer enclosure so the question of the site of the borough remains unresolved.

The castle is in every way remarkable, not least the outer curtain which is laid out geometrically: two long parallel sides with three short straight lengths at either end. If the design of the central block has been correctly identified (figs 57, 58) this represents a monastic

57.   Sherborne old castle, Dorset: an aerial view showing the remarkable outer enclosure and inner claustral courtyard: the two-storeyed chapel facing the ground-floor hall (Cambridge Collection)

precinct wall. There are two mural towers and two long extended gateways over the ditch (figs 57, 58).

If the external wall surprises us the central block of buildings astonishes us even more. It is set slightly towards the north side of the enclosure and consists of four ranges around a courtyard. The northern one was a two-storeyed chapel and the southern parallel one can be identified as a single-storeyed hall.[2] The parallel with church and refectory (frater) in a Benedictine cloister is at once clear, made even more marked by the southern range being now identified as single-storeyed by Alan Cook. The keep with central division adjoins the hall at the south-west corner. In a Benedictine cloister the west range was the abbot's house and the east range, also two-storeyed, was of course the monks' dormitory. The ranges could be used in the same way here and I have little doubt that the inspiration of the design is a Benedictine cloister.

The 1130s were a period of intense castle and monastic founda-tion, so many examples were at hand. What could be the motiva-

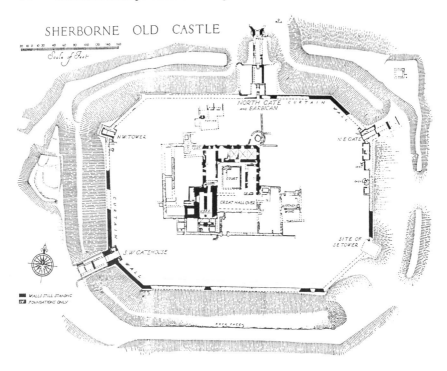

58.   Sherborne old castle: detailed plan by RCHME. The hall was not
'over' but on the ground floor. The castle is apparently of one design

tion? Roger, unlike Henry of Blois, had no monastic background: he
was a secular. Whether a castle in this form might give less offence,
suggesting as it does some kind of conventual life, important for a
high ecclesiastic, is a matter for discussion. What is clear is that even
in is ruinous state it is something of a high water mark in episcopal
secular architecture: originality is not a marked quality of prelates.

At Old Sarum castle the enclosure already existed in the royal
castle and there may also have been existing buildings, so Bishop
Roger did not have a free hand in the way he did at Sherborne.
Nevertheless it is clearly the same principle at work, with the hall/
frater this time on the north and the keep projecting from the
enclosure. We do not know whether Bishop Roger tried to construct
similar courtyards at Malmesbury and Devizes but it seems clear
that none of the other bishops tried to build anything similar, nor
indeed did any other castle builder.

ii   Henry of Blois, bishop of Winchester (1129–71)

The next *episcopus potentissimus*, to use the term employed in the *Historia Novella*, to whom attention must be paid is Henry of Blois. More famed to posterity than Roger, he had a German biography devoted to him in 1932 (Voss). Although he was certainly inspired by Bishop Roger in the adjoining diocese he was of a different generation, born in the 1090s and so 25–30 years younger. His background was quite different; educated at Cluny he was brought over by Henry I in 1126 to be abbot of Glastonbury. He started as a monk. The combined resources of a wealthy abbey and the wealthiest see from 1129, when he became bishop of Winchester, gave him the opportunity to indulge in widespread constructional activity. His resources were much greater than those of Roger although he never perhaps enjoyed the real authority of the latter, living in much more turbulent times. Nevertheless he died peacefully and was not overtaken by disaster as happened to Roger.

The main concern here is not with history or biography but with Henry's castles. Fortunately Hampshire County Council have just published an excellent account of his buildings with a map (Riall, 1994) to which the reader may be referred. First it is necessary to return to Winchester.

Wolvesey has been briefly discussed (p. 44) but the anonymous author of the *Gesta Stephani* clearly states that apart from Wolvesey, tucked away in the south-east corner of the town, Henry had a castle 'which he had built in a very elegant style in the middle of the town' (Potter, 1955a, 84). Giraldus Cambrensis may mean that he used the material from the royal houses for building here (Dimock, 1877, 46). This is surely where the *turris fortissima* was, from which missiles were thrown into the town, that the Winchester annalist put into Wolvesey. Only this way can the events described be intelligible. No trace of the castle in the town remains. The annalist could not conceive that the bishop would build a castle at the see, so he speaks of a *domus*. He had no difficulty in naming five castles built by Henry on the manors: Merdon, Hants; Farnham, Surrey; Bishops Waltham, Hants; Downton, Wilts; and Taunton, Somerset. There are substantial masonry or earthwork remains at all five places.

The manor sites chosen for castle development were probably not selected at random but wherever it seemed likely that a borough would develop. Of the five Waltham and Merdon did not achieve this but Farnham and Downton did, while Taunton, already a

59.   Farnham castle, Surrey: seat of the bishops of Winchester, an aerial view. Note outer curtain, Waynflete's brick tower, hall block, encased motte and stump of square keep within mound, the *folie de grandeur* of Henry of Blois (RCHME)

borough, no doubt had its status enhanced (*EMB*, 158, 168, 178). All the castles had a setback when, after the bishop's unauthorized absence on the Continent, Henry II seized and destroyed them (*pessum dedit*) (Luard, 1864, ii, 237). Probably only Downton did not recover, although the bishop had a residence there even in the later middle ages.

Farnham castle, Surrey, a favourite residence of the bishops throughout the middle ages up to this century has the most substantial remains (Thompson, 1961). There is an outer enclosure with wall and square towers, and a gatehouse of later date than Henry of Blois. There is a triangular group of buildings in the middle, a motte encased in masonry to the north with attached courtyard below (figs 59, 60). There were probably at least two stages of building: at first a two-storeyed hall, to judge by the chiselled-off arcading on the south wall face, and then later an aisled hall with wooden

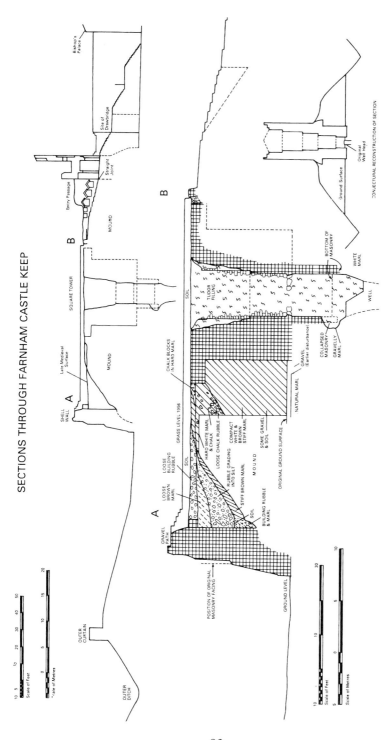

SECTIONS THROUGH FARNHAM CASTLE KEEP

60. Farnham castle: section through the mound showing base of tower with well in the middle, mound later encased and conjectural reconstruction of original tower as built (M.W. Thompson)

93

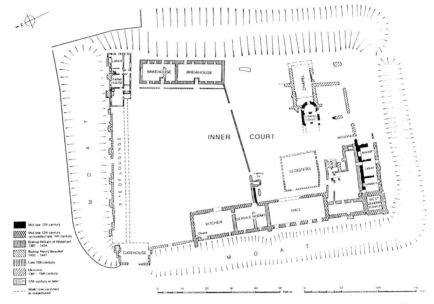

61. Bishops Waltham, Hants: dated plan of buildings within moated area. Note chapel sequence and the extent of late medieval alteration and addition as in lodgings at north end (Hare)

arcade, a capital of one of the posts surviving in a cupboard. The chapel stood on the west corner. However the sequence is by no means clear. The front entry is beneath the great brick tower with portcullis built by Bishop Waynflete in 1470–75 (p. 6). The discovery in 1958 that the mound of the motte enclosed a great square tower base, enlarged by 2 m at the top in a sort of flange over the beaten chalk marl of the mound, constructed *pari passu* with the tower, transformed our view of the early, presumably Henry of Blois', castle. Evidently a massive tower 16 m square rose from the mound and was presumably demolished by the king in 1155. Quite possibly a wooden base supported a wooden superstructure as a normal method in such mounds but to do it in stone suggests a *folie de grandeur* very much in keeping with the bishop's character as described by Giraldus (Thompson, 1960; Dimock, 1877, vii, 43–5).

Taunton castle is in the centre of the modern town. It had a keep, inner ward and larger outer enclosure known as the bailey, perhaps the original borough. Excavations (Radford and Hallason, 1952) have revealed a massive plinth possibly enclosing an earlier motte

62.   Bishops Waltham: the 12th-century keep, probably late Henry of Blois but much altered later as were adjoining buildings (A.E. Thompson)

and some interesting alterations in the domestic buildings. How much is to be attributed to Henry of Blois is not clear. There seems to have been the usual change from first-floor to ground-floor hall.

Bishops Waltham differs very markedly from Farnham castle, Surrey, and is indeed hardly entitled to the name of castle at all (figs 61, 62). It is a rectangular moated area, the abundant water supply perhaps making a more regular form possible than a hilltop site. It has been the subject of research over many years, excavation and more recently study of the manorial accounts (Hare, 1988). The earliest buildings in the south west of the enclosure comprised a keep and 'great chamber' and hall with services along the west side.

To the east is the apsidal end of a two-storeyed chapel replaced in the fifteenth century by another. It is agreed that the early work cannot go back to the 1130s and should be by Henry of Blois after the slighting of the first castle in 1155. Traces of early remains have been found to the north of the moated area; it is assumed that Henry's earlier castle was an earthwork that has been destroyed. It underwent a major transformation during the episcopates of William Wykeham (1367–1404) and Cardinal Beaufort (1405–47) which included the construction of a long two-storeyed range of cellular lodgings at its northern end.

The last two of Bishop Henry's castles at Merdon and Downton survive as earthworks although at Merdon there is masonry including a probable keep.[3]

The recent discoveries by the Oxford Archaeological Unit at Witney, Oxon, consist of a rectangular masonry structure, 7 by 11 m internally. The walls are not of keep thickness and this, combined with ground floor loops and a central block perhaps to support a central hearth above, possibly indicate some kind of 'protokeep' although it has not the unequal division we associate with that (Durham, 1985). It need not belong to the time of Henry of Blois although coins seem to support this. A view of 1729 by Nathaniel Buck reproduced in the interim report shows a substantial twelfth-century building with pilasters but evidently not what was found in the excavation. It reminds one of the square structure at Norwich terminating Losinga's hall and to judge by his reconstruction the author thinks in similar terms. There is another foundation, possibly of a chapel. The lesson of Witney is: what other large buildings lie concealed on the Winchester manors awaiting discovery and not referred to by the chroniclers? It is doubtful if Witney can be classified as a castle although the rectangular structure comes near to being a keep so is included here. Bitterne, near Southampton, may have had a castle if Leland is to be trusted (Leland, i, 280).

iii   Alexander, bishop of Lincoln (1123–48)

Bishops Alexander of Lincoln and Nigel of Ely are coupled together in the chronicles as 'nephews' of Bishop Roger of Salisbury, although it is only to the former that specific castles are attributed. Unlike Henry of Blois they probably owed their advancement to Bishop Roger and clearly were greatly influenced by him (he was

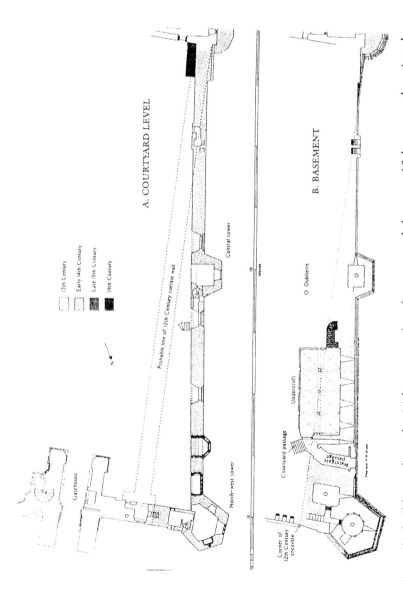

A. COURTYARD LEVEL

12th Century
Early 14th Century
Late 15th Century
19th Century

N

Probable line of 12th Century curtain wall

Gatehouse

Central tower

North-west tower

50

Metres

0

B. BASEMENT

O Oubliette

Courtyard passage

Undercroft

Watergate passage

Corner of
12th Century
enceinte

63. Newark castle: buildings along the 14th-century river frontage and the great 12th-century keep/gatehouse of Bishop Alexander facing the highway to the bridge (Marshall and Samuels)

64.   Newark: an 18th-century view across the river Trent towards the castle showing its close connection with the bridge even later

possibly their natural father). We have already met Alexander at Lincoln who moved from the royal castle or its annex to the Roman East Gate (p. 22). The Winchester annalist puts him down as fortifying Lincoln castle so he may still have had an interest in the royal castle (Luard, 1864, ii, 51). This is a fairly generalized reference, but the three new castles specifically attributed to Alexander are Newark, Notts, Banbury, Oxon and Sleaford, Lincs.

Newark has very substantial remains almost literally overhanging the river Trent; the replacement of the earlier house by the castle went hand in hand with the construction of a new bridge over the river which allowed the Great North Road to be diverted across it.[4] It was a long established borough (*EMB*, 146) and tolls no doubt could be charged for the bridge so there was a commercial interest. The main monument is the great gateway keep which has been compared with the gateways at Sherborne. Recent excavations by Pamela Marshall have demonstrated that the Norman river curtain was moved forward towards the river in the fourteenth century (figs 63, 64).

At Newark the intention of building a castle at the bridgehead was evidently to enhance an existing borough but at Banbury, Oxon, the object was to create a new one (Harvey in Lobel, 1969) as it was at (New) Sleaford where it was again associated with a bridge (Beresford, 1967, 406). Only earthen mounds are visible at either site but at Banbury excavation has shown a square enclosure later made concentric by an outer defence (Rodwell, 1976). We know from the registers that Sleaford castle was in active use into the later middle ages.

Bishop Alexander's castles, like those of Bishop Roger, were confiscated in 1139 and it was at this time that the question of the possible infraction of canon law by bishops building or rather retaining castles ('render unto Caesar... ') arose (Kealey, 1972, 195). Whether this had anything to do with the virtual cessation of the foundation of new castles by bishops after that time must be a matter for discussion.

iv   Hugh du Puiset, bishop of Durham (1153–95)

Hitherto we have dealt with southern or midland dioceses: Salisbury, Winchester, Lincoln and Ely. Puiset had a direct link with the south as he owed his election to the see of Durham to Henry of Blois whose 'nephew' he was (Voss, 1932, 68–9). The times were very unfavourable in the reign of Henry II for the unauthorized building of castles. Puiset was a considerable builder on the manors and at Durham castle, but the only castle with which his name is closely associated is Norham castle in Northumberland on the Scottish border, where defence was of course of paramount importance.

The whole sequence at Norham has recently been worked out by Dixon and Marshall (1993). It is a remarkable story. The first building, the larger part of the keep which is divided into two unequal parts, was a two-storeyed hall with transverse arches and groined vault over the ground floor (figs 65, 66). This is attributed not to Puiset but to Bishop Flambard (1099–1128). The only odd feature is that the southern wall is thinner than its northern, although both would have been external walls. At Chepstow, Gwent, the eleventh-century inner protected wall is much thinner than the wall facing out, no doubt to resist missiles better, and there might be a similar explanation here. The narrow southern compartment with its barrel vault and windows at two levels would be Puiset's addi-

65. Norham, Northumberland: the first stage of the keep as a two-storeyed hall as envisaged by Dixon and Marshall (1993) attributable to Bishop Flambard of Durham (1099–1128)

tion of 40 years later, who also raised the building to its present height. There were further alterations in the fifteenth century. The whole story is worked out with great skill by the authors and is a remarkable account of the transformation of a small two-storeyed hall into a keep. The curtain wall and gatehouse would also be attributable to Puiset (fig. 67).

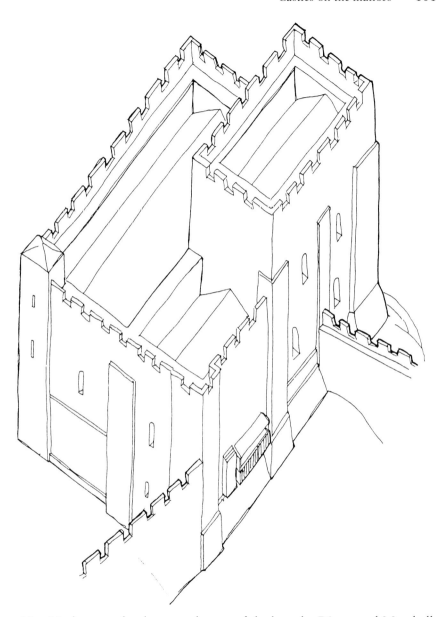

66.   Norham castle: the second stage of the keep by Dixon and Marshall, enlarged and raised by Puiset

The remarkable feature of this great outburst of episcopal castle-building in the first half of the twelfth century is that it was con-fined to three dioceses: Salisbury, Winchester and Lincoln. The

67. Norham castle: aerial view showing keep and inner and outer wards with remains of domestic buildings (Cambridge Collection)

archbishops had no part in it, nor indeed the other bishops; the chroniclers would hardly have passed over in silence work of this kind in other dioceses. In a list of castles based on written sources

(Brown, 1959) in 1154–1216 out of 327 castles 18 belonged to bishops and only Bishop's Stortford, Essex, Eccleshall, Staffs, and Bishop's Castle, Salop, with Durham, Norham, Northallerton and Tweedmouth in the Durham diocese were not in the four dioceses (including Ely to take account of Bishop Nigel) involved.

The underlying motive in most cases was to create or enhance a borough, a favoured speculative venture of the period. Sometimes it turned out a success and sometimes not. Bishop Roger was certainly the most original of the three, Bishops Henry and Alexander being fairly traditional in ideas even taking into account the *folie de grandeur* of the suspended tower at Farnham. Alexander was perhaps the most successful in terms of boroughs that throve.

Notes

1. RCHME, *Dorset*, 1, 66; the plan is at 72–3.
2. Lecture by Alan Cook on recent work at the castle at the Society of Antiquaries, 6 February 1997.
3. *VCH, Hants*, iii, 418 and see photograph in Riall, 1994, 16.
4. Braun, 1935; superseded by Marshall and Samuels, 1997, who regard the Norman curtain as further from the river.

6   *Episcopal security in the later middle ages*

i   Crime and violence

Our picture of the state of society in the later middle ages has been considerably altered in the last few years by the historians. Attitudes towards the middle ages have always been ambivalent: 'medieval' in ordinary speech can be pejorative but for many Victorians it meant the age of faith and Gothic architecture. It comes as no surprise therefore that Pike in his *History of Crime* (1873, chapter 4) when he studied 'England before the Black Death' from Court rolls was horrified at what he found. The level of violent crime was almost beyond belief, making one think of modern Sicily or Chicago during Prohibition. Needless to say the matter was not pursued until recently when a number of historians (eg Hilton, 1996; Bellamy, 1973) have turned their attention to it.

The study of the Coterel gang (Bellamy, 1964) reveals the state of affairs in the midlands in 1327–33. What is so remarkable is the extent to which all levels of society, including the clergy, were involved. Crime was pervasive.

Several facts have been established about the level of crime (Bellamy, 1973). First that it fluctuated, its level being closely related to the exercise of authority of the king. The chief law enforcement officers, the Sheriffs, were agents of the king, and a weak or ineffective or absent king led to a deterioration and rise in crime. Thus the long absences of Edward I (1272–1307) in Wales and Scotland seems to have led to a noticeable deterioration. The subsequent periods of civil strife and ineffective monarchs led to periods of recrudescence of lawlessness in the fourteenth and fifteenth centuries. 'Violence was part of the pattern of life in the later middle ages and men did not shed tears over it easily' as Bellamy remarked (*ibid.*, 37).

Margaret Paston wrote to her husband probably in 1461 (letter 432):

> Wherefor like it you be the more war of your gyddyng for your persones saufgard, and also that ye be not to hasty to come into this cuntre til ye here the world more sewer

Bishops were not particularly dishonest with one very probable exception, Bishop Thomas de Lisle of Ely, who has been the subject of an excellent biography (Aberth, 1996) which incidentally also has a lot to say about late medieval crime: 'the peace is very troubled and disturbed and the law hindered and almost ignored' (Parliament in 1348). This is quoted from Aberth and is one of several such complaints from Parliament. The bishop had a long dispute in the courts with Lady Wake and in the course of this the lady's steward was murdered with or without the complicity of the bishop. He had a narrow escape in 1356 when, emerging from his house at Somersham, his party was harassed by a mob led by the sister of the murdered man. Caught in the traffic at St Ives the bishop and his party had to abandon their wagons and flee on horseback to his manor at Little Gransden. The point about the story is that it was no use fleeing to a nearby manor unless it had minimum defences such as a moat to keep the mob out (fig. 68).

Four bishops met a violent end in the period: Walter Stapleton (Exeter), murdered by the mob in 1326 and his body flung on a rubbish heap; Archbishop Sudbury, executed by the rebels on Tower hill in 1381; during Cade's rebellion Adam Moleyns (Chichester) and William Ayscough (Salisbury), the latter dragged from the church at Edington while celebrating mass and the corpse flung into a field.[1] These were mob murders, sometimes politically engineered. In the case of Ayscough the murder at nearby Edington caused worries in Wells close, prompting renewal of the licence to crenellate. The other prelate to die violently was Archbishop Scrope of York, tried and executed for treason at Bishopsthorpe in 1405. It reflects a changed attitude towards the episcopate that this could happen.

With respect to bishops there are two further factors that cannot be ignored. The first arises from the position of the bishops as landowners and their consequent relationship to the peasantry who worked the land for them. 'Peasant resistance to seigneurial pressure seems first to become significant in England in the thirteenth century' (Hilton, 1990, 54). This is partly due to the proliferation of the relevant documents at that time. Hilton attributed this to increased labour services on demesne land required by higher agricultural production. Certainly the surviving custumals for the bishop of Chichester's manors in 1243–4 do suggest burdensome labour services (Peckham, 1925). However it is not economic history that is the concern of this book, not the causes so much as the effects.

THE WEST VIEW OF BUCKDEN PALACE, IN THE COUNTY OF HUNTINGDON.

To the Right Rev.d Father in God RICH.IRD.
Lord Bishop of Lincoln, Owner of this Palace.
This Prospect is humbly Inscribed by.
Y.r Lordships,
Most Obed.t & Dutiful Serv.ts
Sam: & Nath: Buck.

THIS Beautifull brick Palace and its Manor belong'd formerly to the Way of Eto which was then on the Diocess of Lincoln, until Richard the last West of nan Leave of K. Hen. 8.to turn this Way of Ely into a Cathedral,and to make himself by this means first Bishop thereof; but this not being to be done without giving up that Diocess he was oblig'd to purchase instead this Prio of three Manors in this ma once in process of Time became a Palace and Residence of the Bp. of Lincoln as it now continues Manor & of Ely remained the 1546 built great part of its appears by his Arms over Palace,land was created Ed.ter of historie,much cost as appears & beautifying it. Arms orsmeninic is Bp of Lincoln by Patents 5 July 6.th

118

106

68.   Buckden, Huntingdonshire: a Bucks' view of 1730 of a favoured residence of the bishops of Lincoln. Note the moat, the great brick tower and very high level of late medieval fortification

What had been aggressive action against the bishops in the courts led in due time to rioting and in due course to the great rebellion of 1381. The coordination over large areas in 1381 suggests a long history of cooperation. Among the earlier riots those at Bury St Edmunds in 1327 with three attacks on the monastery, in which 20,000 men and women are said to have taken part and fourteen manors to have been destroyed (Yates, 1843) were bad. Monks were beaten, buildings damaged and documents destroyed. As later in 1381, 'the rebels saw the documents as the means by which rents and labour services had been increased'. The military had to be summoned. In 1381 the town was even more seriously affected, the Chief Justice and the Prior being publicly beheaded (*ibid.*, 136).

Rioting was endemic: in Oxford in 1354 students and townsmen clashed for several days with several fatalities and Cambridge had its share particularly in 1381 when Corpus Christi was left ransacked; while Canterbury had riots in the 1320s and 1340s, in 1342 the close being attacked (Rogers, 1891; Powell, 1896, 9; Hilton and Ashton, 1984, 121–4). There was an insecurity in life with which today we are quite unfamiliar.

Were bishops especially vulnerable to anti-clericalism? There is no doubt from the pages of Chaucer, Langland and Wycliffe that it was the regulars who particularly aroused wrath, the secular priesthood much less. Events in 1381 confirm this since there were priests among the rebels. However, the description of events in 1381 in the *Anonomaille Chronicle* (Galbraith, 1927) leaves little doubt about the prevalence of anti-clericalism. In the next century Gascoigne (Rogers, 1881, 15ff) thought the bishops had largely brought their troubles on their own heads through absenteeism, neglect of pastoral duty, life of luxury and so on, leading up to the murder of the bishops. Grosseteste was held up as an example of how a bishop should behave. While bishops had perhaps been more worldly than before, it must be doubtful if they were more vulnerable than lay lords although not protected by their office as they might have been in the twelfth century: the murder of Archbishop Sudbury did not arouse the same feelings as did the murder of Thomas Becket 200 years earlier.

ii   Licences to crenellate

The value of licences to crenellate (authority to fortify a property from the Crown recorded on the back of the Patent Rolls) for dating buildings was first recognized by J. H. Parker in the last century who published a list of them (Turner and Parker, iv, 410–21). From a list expanded by Dr Charles Coulson I have extracted the episcopal licences to crenellate (see page 167). Anthony Emery has made a study of all the licences and drawn up block diagrams showing their occurrence by decades (Emery, 1996, 172–80). They are confined mainly to the period 1260–1400 with a trickle up to the sixteenth century and a few in the earlier thirteenth century. The climax is in the middle of the fourteenth century. It is clear many people did not bother with the expense and fuss of having a copy on the Patent Roll. Some lords, as in Durham where it was the bishop, had their own right to license.

In the twelfth century castles were primarily regarded as fortresses for fighting between social equals; in the later middle ages fortification was largely against social inferiors, in England at all events. Social equals fought each other in the open field. No doubt there were exceptions: in the conquest of Wales or Ireland the native population was to some extent the enemy. In the later middle ages the enemy was at the gate, but ill-armed and ill-equipped; he was not a military enemy to be fought, but to be overawed by fierce-looking buildings, even if some parts like opposing gunports were not functional. It was one reason for the theatrical element in the military architecture (fig. 68).

The licences are not therefore normally for castles but often for buildings that would have been left unfortified in the twelfth century. The most conspicuous examples are cathedral closes: Wells (1286), Exeter (1290), Lichfield (1289), Lincoln (1316, raise wall 1318), Salisbury (1327). At Lincoln there could have been no processional way from castle to west end of the cathedral if the Exchequer gate had been there; the close shut itself off in the fourteenth century. The monastic cathedrals were already enclosed but the secular ones must have much resembled French cathedrals before the fourteenth century. Even the monastic cathedrals strengthened their fortifications, as at Norwich or Ely.

The need for protection of the close may be illustrated by Lichfield in the hundred years before the Reformation (Kettle, 1985). The close gates were meticulously closed at night and in 1436 a party of

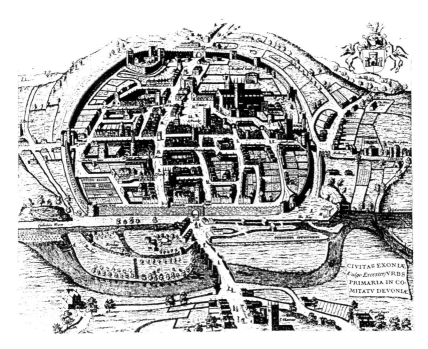

69.   Exeter: a 17th-century view from the south with river in the foreground. Note the fortified bishop's palace south-east of the cathedral and surviving fragments of the close wall

townsmen tried to break them down. There was constant friction with the town. More serious was the case of Norwich. In 1272 before the enclosure of the close a letter of Pope Gregory upbraided the citizens for pursuing fugitives into the monastic precinct and doing much damage. In 1443 the Priory was attacked under the leadership of the mayor using artillery and trying to undermine the gates (Hudson and Tingey, 1906, 60, 340).

Houses that might have been virtually undefended in the twelfth century or early thirteenth century suddenly acquired moats, gate-houses, walls and towers. This applies mainly to manor houses but also to London, as Langton's house by Temple Bar (1305) or Booth's house at Battersea (1474). Numerous excavators have reported how on manor sites a vague spread of buildings suddenly reorganized itself within a moat. The see palace at Wells is a good example, where the zig-zag early buildings do not relate at all to the moat and later fortifications (figs 30, 31).

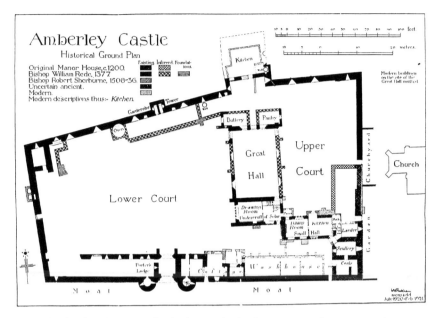

70.   Amberley, Sussex: the bishop of Chichester's modest manor house transformed after a licence of 1377 into a castle with a large hall and lodging ranges, prompted by French raids on south coast (Peckham)

The places where there was a serious outside enemy were no doubt fortified for quite different reasons: La Rose, the main seat of Carlisle's bishop (1336 and 1355) which had been burnt by the Scots; Amberley castle, Sussex (1377) (fig. 70), where the bishop of Chichester was vulnerable to French raids, and his twelve manor houses in Sussex (1477).

The period of soaring crime identified by the social historians starts in c. 1270 and it is surely no accident that the licences to crenellate suddenly appear at the same time. Why they should have risen so dramatically in the middle of the next century is not clear, but perhaps the savage rioting at Bury St Edmunds in 1327 encouraged the view that a licence was prudent. Our problem is that we do not know what proportion of work was licensed and what was done without formality, probably the larger part. The numbers of licences then begins to fall in the fifteenth century when it was regarded more as an unnecessary and expensive formality. The firm hand of Tudor government with the prerogative courts raised security to a much higher level, so that fortification was no longer needed.

71.   Charing, Kent: the undefended entry of c.1300 to the archbishop's manor house adjoining the parish church. Cf. figs 68, 72 (A.E. Thompson)

After the rebellion of 1381, in 1382 the Augustinian priory of Thornton in north Lincolnshire obtained a licence to build a great gatehouse (*CPR*, 1382, 166), and we see the result in the huge structure that exists today, set on the circuit of a strong wall with a large moat in front. At Bury St Edmunds the response to the 1327 riot was to build the fine gatehouse that we see there today. The great gatehouses of abbeys, often all that survives, are among the principal late medieval monuments in the country (St Albans, Battle, St Osyth, St Augustines at Canterbury and so on). They are not really fortified and the object presumably was to overawe and disperse a gathering mob; they also constituted a safe archive for the records which as the events in 1381 demonstrated were what the mob wished to burn. No doubt also they provided some refuge if the mob managed to enter the monastery. Almost as vulnerable were the colleges of universities: it is instructive to compare the innocuous fourteenth-century entry in the range of Pembroke, Cambridge, with the later great towered entries at Queens, Kings Old Court or St Johns to see intentions similar to those at the monasteries at work.

72.   Knole, Kent: the huge gateway into the archbishop's 15th-century house, quite disproportionate to the domestic function of the building (A.E. Thompson)

In the cathedral closes similar gates exist and also at the palace itself, as the Alnwick tower at Lincoln. On the manors gatehouses appear but not on the scale of the abbeys (figs 71, 72). Cardinal Morton's tower at Lambeth has a pedestrian and carriage entry but is in the same family. Morton was not a popular man. There are gates at Esher, altered by Kent, half a great gate at Otford and of course at Hampton Court.

The visitor coming up the hill at Farnham, Surrey, is indeed impressed by the great brick tower hovering over the town (p. 6, fig. 3). Built in 1470–5 by Waynflete (Thompson, 1960) its appearance has been altered by the insertion of sash windows, but even with the original windows it can hardly have been a very forbidding building. Moulded brick was used freely in it and there is a groove for a portcullis. The staircase for the first floor is in a projection on the north side. The main interest at Farnham, however, is that unlike a monastic gatehouse it was a residence set at the lower end of the hall allowing the service of food from the kitchen to it. It provides a kind of link between the true gatehouse and the free-standing brick tower at Buckden, Hunts, a favourite residence of the

73.   Buckden, Hunts: aerial view of the bishop of Lincoln's house. Cf.
fig. 68. The great brick tower of Bishop Rotherham (1472–80) survives
close to the parish church (Cambridge Collection)

bishops of Lincoln. It was probably built by Bishop Rotherham
(1472–80), again brick but with stone dressings. Standing immediately beside the parish church it was an impressive structure (figs
68, 73, 74). The foundations of the thirteenth-century hall have
been revealed by excavation. These keep-like towers are borrowed
from the secular lords, particularly Lord Cromwell's tower of thirty
years earlier at Tattershall, Lincolnshire. It should be noted none of
these decidedly assertive structures were licensed.

It would be a serious mistake to regard the bishops as passive in
the social confrontation of the period. In 1381 Henry Despenser
(1370–1406) took the lead against the insurgents in East Anglia and
put them down with a firm hand (Powell, 1896, 55). In 1387 he was
licensed to crenellate at North Elmham and Gaywood, Norfolk. In
the former case he transformed a church, probably then disused,
into a sort of fortress (fig. 75). The hall stood on the first floor over
the nave and he duplicated a stair turret to create a fortified gateway (Rigold, 1963). William Courtenay who succeeded Sudbury

74.   Buckden: close-up view of south side of the tower in figs 68 and 73
(A.E. Thompson)

after his murder set about reconstructing Saltwood castle, Kent, the
most conspicuous feature being the astonishingly tall residential
gatehouse built over and against the twelfth-century gatehouse as
can be seen in the aerial photograph (fig. 76).

iii   Castles

It would be a mistake to believe that bishops regarded castles as no
longer serving any useful purpose in the later middle ages, or at least
in the majority of sees this was not so. Norwich, Rochester, Exeter,

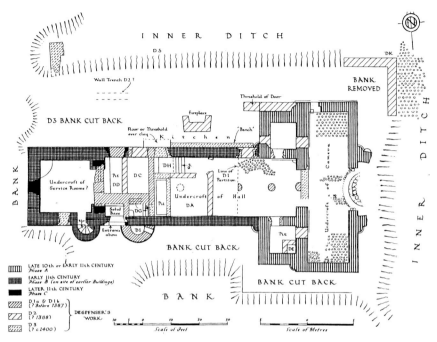

75.   North Elmham, Norfolk: in 1387 a licence authorized Bishop
Despenser of Norwich to transform an existing enigmatic chapel into a
fortress, the nave becoming the undercroft of the hall, the transepts the
chamber, all surrounded by a great ditch (S.E. Rigold)

Bath and Wells, St Asaph and Bangor contrived to manage without
one. Most retained at least one in an inhabitable and presumably
more or less defensible state. It is worth looking at the different sees
starting in the north.

Carlisle

The unfortunate bishop badly needed a good castle. In 1337 the
Scots had sacked Rose and the bishop petitioned the king 'for
custody of Carlisle castle for the term of his life in peace and war…
The bishop has no retreat in his bishopric and wishes to make a
fortlet' (Storey, 1995, 82–3). The king did not agree and only allowed the bishop temporary refuge in it. There were licences to
crenellate for the Rose in 1336 and 1355 when it was rebuilt. The
Rose, much altered, remains the residence of the bishop to the present
day. At the time of the Scottish incursions the registers show that

76.   Saltwood castle, Kent: Archbishop Courtenay largely rebuilt the 12th-century castle, particularly the domestic buildings including a high residential gate tower in front of the earlier gatehouse (Cambridge Collection)

John Kirkby lived mainly at his manors of Horncastle, Lincs, and Melbourne, Derbys., valuable places of retreat.

Durham

The bishop had the castle by the cathedral, which remained in use, although in the fourteenth century he seemed to use the castles at Stockton on Tees and Bishops Middleham, Co. Durham, and Crayke castle in North Yorkshire. Howden and Ricall in the East Riding were favourite manors. The bishop's present residence at Bishop Auckland (erroneously called a castle) had come into use in at least the thirteenth century. This contains the famous hall (figs 34, 35) attributed, probably wrongly, to Puiset and converted into a chapel at the Restoration. At right angles is the two-storeyed rectangular building with vaulted ground floor of Anthony Bek (1286–1311). Compared with Carlisle, Durham had a surfeit of castles.

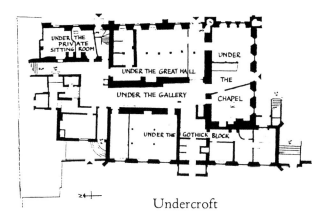

Undercroft

Bishopthorpe Palace
Principal Floor

77.   Bishopthorpe, Yorkshire: the archbishop's palace at ground and first-floor levels. Note the 13th-century first-floor hall and compare Worcester, Wells and Salisbury (Gee)

York

In complete contrast to Durham the archbishop does not seem to have had any castle until Cawood was licensed in 1272. Although only the gatehouse and adjoining wall survives Leland described it as 'a very fair castel' and he was no mean judge (Leland, iv, 12). Cawood and Bishopthorpe, the modern seat of the archbishop, seem to have been the favourite residences (fig. 77). Could Little Compton, Warwicks (licence 1291), have been a refuge for St Davids like Melbourne and Horncastle for the bishop of Carlisle or Pleasley, Derbys. (licence 1285)? The archbishop had a number of manors further south, notably Southwell, Notts.

Lincoln

Of Bishop Alexander's castles the one that remained in continuous use was Sleaford. The most favoured manors were Buckden, Hunts, Lyddington, Rutland and Stow Park, Lincs. At Lyddington a long range (possibly the original hall block) adjoins the parish church and contains a fine fifteenth-century ceiling in what must then have been a great chamber. At right angles to this the foundations of a large broad hall have been discovered recently (C. and P. Woodfield, 1988) which apparently had an earlier smaller stage (fig. 78).

Coventry and Lichfield

Eccleshall castle, Staffs, has a very early licence of 1200 restraining efforts to prevent enclosure. However, it was rebuilt as a two-storeyed block, known from late seventeenth-century drawings as perhaps more of a fortified house than a castle, by Bishop Walter Langton presumably at the same time as he constructed the formidable close wall at Lichfield and fortified his London house, licence 1305 (Maddison, 1993). Eccleshall castle was in active use with Heywood, Staffs, the main manor house, followed by Prees, Shropshire, Sawley, Derbyshire and Tarvin, Cheshire.

Worcester

Hartlebury castle was started by Bishop Cantilupe (1236–66) and completed by Giffard. There is a licence of 1268 (not enrolled). The alterations are so complete that only the general shape indicates that

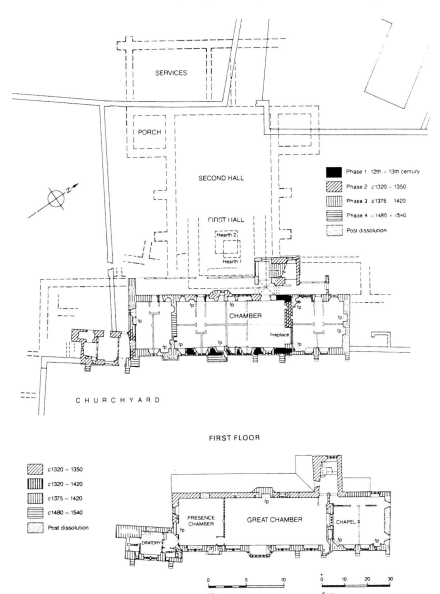

78.   Lyddington, Rutland: range with great chamber (later bede house) adjoining the church and two stages of a vanished ground-floor hall set at right angles identified by C. and P. Woodfield

it must have been a hall with wings, a house in fact. Part of a mural tower indicates more extensive fortification. The original thirteenth-century chapel survives. Among favoured manor houses were Alvechurch, Kempsey, Bredon in Worcestershire, Weston Subedge and Withington in Gloucestershire and Itchell (Crondall), Hampshire border on the way to London.

Hereford

Bishops Castle, Lydney North, Shropshire, is right on the Welsh border and was kept in use through the middle ages. Bosbury and Stretton Sugwas in the county and Prestbury, Glos, were the main manor houses.

Llandaff

The castle by the cathedral was abandoned in the early fifteenth century in favour of Mathern, Gwent (Johns, 1974).

St Davids

Llawhaden castle, built originally as an enclosure with round towers, was entirely reconstructed in c. 1300 with rectangular towers and projecting rooms, all at first-floor level in Welsh fashion (fig. 79). Although the status of Swansea castle has been a matter for discussion, Leland's remarks support the view that the surviving part was the bishop's.[2] Apart from the ornamental arcading below the parapet of Henry of Gower (p. 62), the buildings themselves, hall and chamber raised over a vault in Welsh fashion are of very considerable interest. For lack of early registers we do not know where the bishop lived. The most impressive manor house is Lamphey, Pembrokeshire (fig. 80), where there are three two-storeyed buildings evidently representing three stages of hall, ending with one with rather coarse Henry Gower-style decoration.[3] There is also a two-storeyed chapel. The licence for Pleasley, Derbyshire, 1285, followed Edward I's second Welsh campaign and may have been to create a refuge.

Ely

The bishops retained the early castle of Wisbech in north Cambridgeshire which was reconstructed late in the middle ages al-

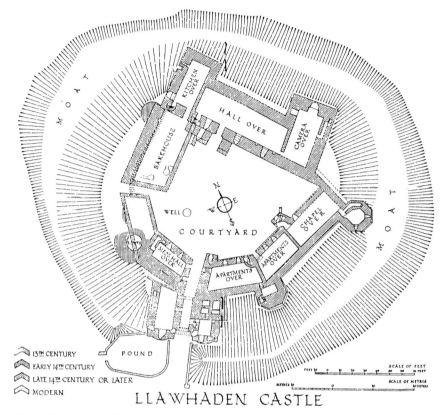

79.   Llawhaden, Pembrokeshire: bishop of St David's castle, first a ringwork, then polygonal with round towers at the angles, replaced in 14th century by rectangular buildings all over basements and finally large gatehouse (Radford)

though virtually nothing is visible now. It has been suggested that Thomas Arundel, bishop 1374–85, took refuge there in the summer of 1381 during the uprising (Aston, 1967, 139). Apart from Wisbech the favoured houses were Downham, Cambs, Somersham, Hunts, and Hatfield, Herts, rebuilt by Morton before his elevation to Canterbury.

Winchester

Farnham castle, Surrey, was occupied throughout the period and used by bishops of Winchester up to this century. Taunton castle

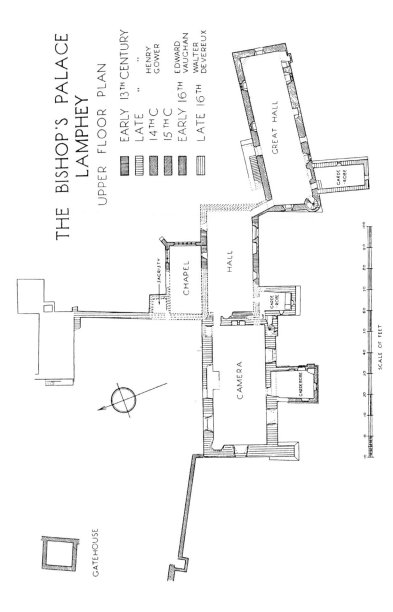

THE BISHOP'S PALACE
LAMPHEY
UPPER FLOOR PLAN

EARLY 13TH CENTURY
LATE   ''
14TH C   HENRY GOWER
15TH C
EARLY 16TH   EDWARD VAUGHAN
LATE 16TH   WALTER DEVEREUX

GATEHOUSE

CAMERA

GARDE ROBE

SACRISTY

CHAPEL

HALL

GARDE ROBE

GREAT HALL

GARDE ROBE

SCALE OF FEET

80. Lamphey, Pembrokeshire: bishop's house with sequence of three first floor halls, the latest evidently Henry of Gower (Radford)

122

was maintained. Bishops Waltham became a most cherished seat at the end of the period but not a castle (p. 13). Other castles fell into decay and were abandoned. Esher, Surrey, Highclere, Waltham and Marwell, Hants, were favoured houses.

Salisbury

Sherborne castle, Dorset (p. 88), which had been confiscated from Bishop Roger in his disgrace in 1139, was restored to the see in the fourteenth century (licence 1337, repeated 1377). Bishops Woodford, Ramsbury, Wilts, and Sonning, Berks (fig. 84) were favoured manors.

London

Bishops Stortford castle, Herts, was an old motte and bailey site but a licence of 1346 confirms its continued maintenance. Among favoured manors were Fulham, the present home of the bishop and rebuilt in the early sixteenth century, Stepney, and Orsett and Bishops Wickham in Essex.

Canterbury

Saltwood castle, Kent, was not used by archbishops in the early period but Courtenay, after his election in 1382, rebuilt it with a tall gate-tower, domestic buildings, chapel and outer curtain. It is not easy to list favoured manor houses since there was a large number widely scattered and they frequently changed.

Chichester

Chichester apparently did not have an early castle but the manor house at Amberley was converted into one following the licence of 1377 (fig. 70). A solid curtain wall encloses a substantial area and the small twelfth-century hall over a vault was replaced by a large hall of which fragments survive. Aldingbourne, Drungeswick (Loxwood) and West Wittering in Sussex were perhaps the most favoured manors.

The four English bishoprics without castles had favoured manors as follows:

Bath and Wells: Banwell, Blackford, Chew Magna, Claverton and Wiveliscombe in Somerset and Dogmersfield, Hants.
Exeter: Bishops Clyst (Farrington), Chudleigh, Clyst Honiton, Bishopsteighton in Devon
Norwich: Blofield, Hoxne in Norfolk, South Elmham, Suff. and Terling, Essex.
Rochester: Halling and Trottiscliffe, Kent.

Surveying the lists above it is clear that those sees with castles maintained and often reconstructed one of them at least, not usually more than one. Those that did not have them did not build one afresh except Chichester where its peculiar vulnerability to French raids required it.

Notes

1. All these bishops are included in the *DNB*.
2. Evans (1983) argues cogently that the new castle at Swansea was not episcopal and Henry of Gower had nothing to do with it, although this is not easy to accept.
3. Radford's dates for Llawhaden and Lamphey are slightly altered in the new Cadw guidebook, 1991.

i   From hall to chamber

Juxta gardinum abbatis fecit aulam magnam et honestam, et aliam aulam minorem ad gabulam ejusdem aulae petra coopertam. Et de domo quae prius aula fuit, cameram ordinari fecit. Et iuxta eandem aulam fieri fecit unam coquinam.
[He made a large and proper hall beside the abbot's garden and the other smaller hall at the gable of this hall had its roof re-covered with stone (tiles). And the building which was the hall before he caused to be changed into the chamber. And next to this hall he caused a new kitchen to be made]
Registrum Malmesburiense, RS (1880), 11, 365. Speaking of William of Colerne, abbot 1260–96

This remarkable, probably unique, description of the replacement of the small, presumably twelfth- or early thirteenth-century first-floor hall by a large new, perhaps aisled, hall deserves close atten-tion. The gable end of the new hall was erected against the old one, a stone building with stone roof, in such a way that the hall on the first floor of the old hall could serve as the chamber to the new one. Here we have both types of hall in classic relationship.

It is evident that this is quite incompatible with Dr Blair's thesis[1] which assumes that the old hall was built as a chamber. The scribe is absolutely categorical that it was a hall and had to be converted to a chamber. Blair's thesis assumes that some or all (?which) of these small halls were chambers. In no case has this been proved. In the face of this implacably hard evidence discussion is not necessary.

While the construction of a new hall often caused the old one to be relegated or elevated to a chamber for the bishop, the cases where they are in physical contact are unusual but there are three examples on bishops' manors where something rather similar may have happened to that described at Malmesbury.

The archbishop had modest accommodation at West Tarring (Wor-thing), Sussex, and the surviving buildings at the manor were stud-ied in detail some 75 years ago (Packham, 1923) (figs 81, 82, 83). The sequence started with a building about 11 by 5.5 m internally, two-storeyed and open to the roof on the first floor. The building was at first freestanding and dated to before 1250, but about 1300

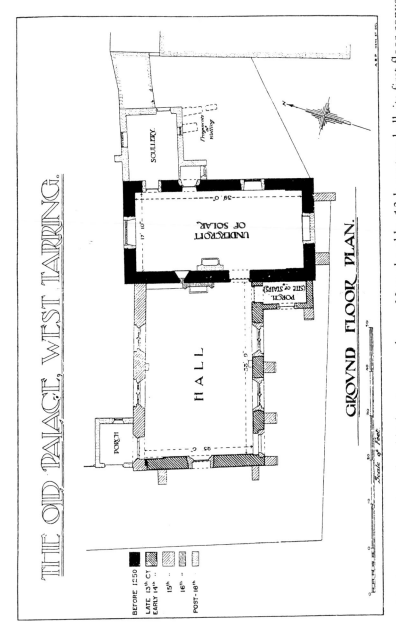

81. West Tarring, Sussex: plan of archbishop's manor house. Note the older 13th-century hall, its first floor converted to solar for new ground-floor hall (Packham)

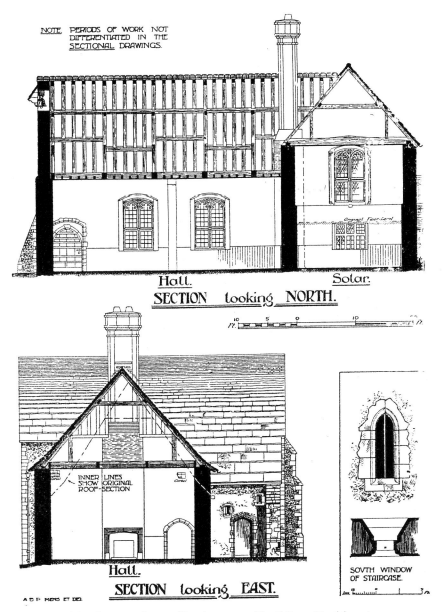

NOTE. PERIODS OF WORK NOT
DIFFERENTIATED IN THE
SECTIONAL DRAWINGS.

Hall.   Solar.
SECTION looking NORTH.

INNER LINES
SHOW ORIGINAL
ROOF-SECTION

Hall.
SECTION looking EAST.

SOVTH WINDOW
OF STAIRCASE.

82.   West Tarring: sections of both parts of building (Packham)

a larger ground-floor building 11 by 8 m (broader but the same length) was built on to it, which underwent various alterations, being widened. The two buildings were called the solar and new hall

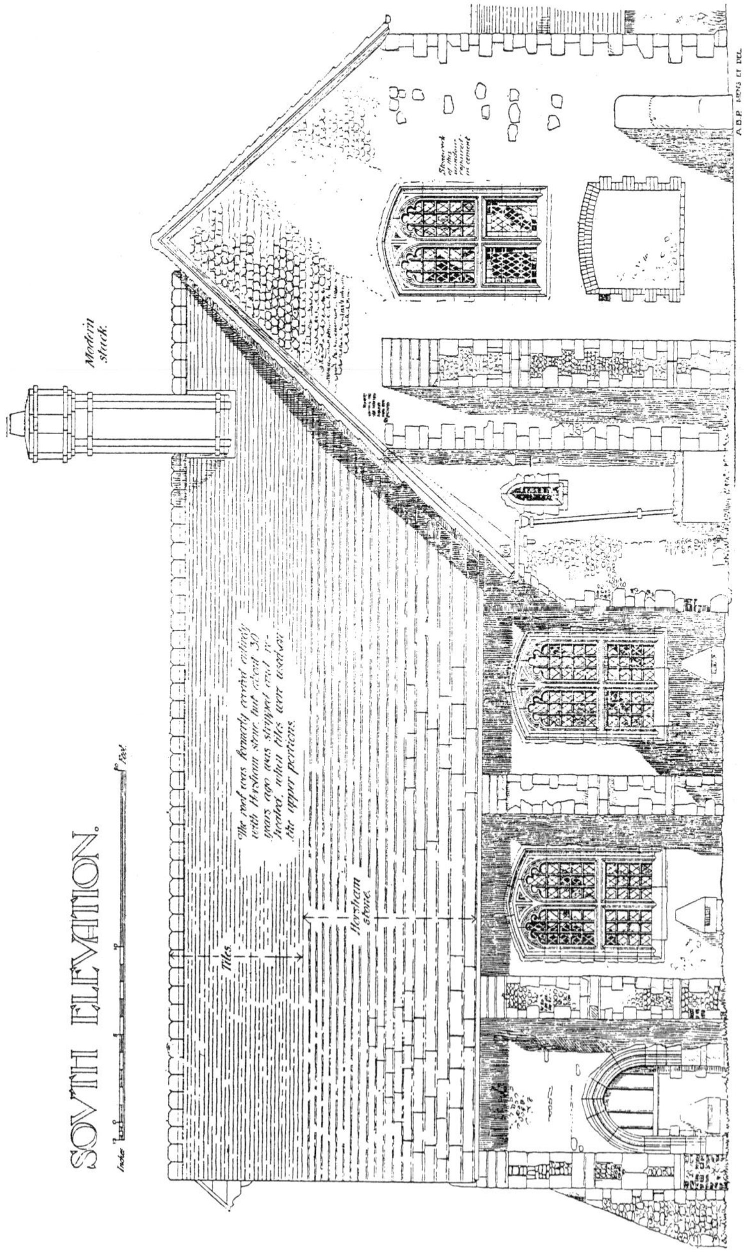

SOUTH ELEVATION.

The roof was formerly corded, ceiling
with Horsham stone but about 30
years ago was stripped and co-
bonded, without tiles were wooden
the upper portions.

Tiles

Horsham brick

Modern stock

83. West Tarring: elevation of south side (Packham)

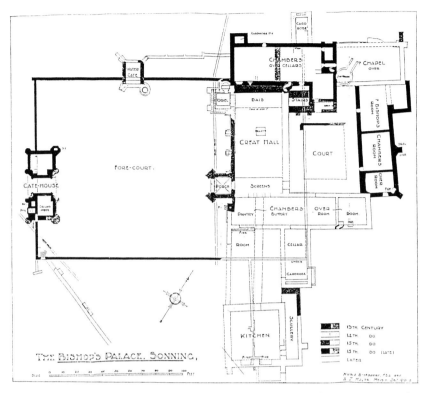

84. Sonning, Berkshire: plan of bishop of Salisbury's house excavated in 1912–13 by Brakspear, showing original hall with undercroft by river replaced by ground-floor hall with central hearth at right angles (Brakspear)

by Packham who studied them but I would prefer to refer to the old hall and new hall as described at Malmesbury.

The bishop of Salisbury had a manor at Sonning, Berkshire, on the route to London where he himself had a house in very active use. The site was excavated by Brakspear just before the First World War, with remarkable results little known because the journal in which they were published (1916), did not survive. A coloured plan, fashionable at that time, records more or less the full area (fig. 84). The original hall by the riverside was set over a vaulted undercroft and measured roughly 19 by 7.5 m internally, extended eastwards in the fourteenth century (the hall was thirteenth century) to a two-storeyed chapel. In the fourteenth century a fine hall measuring about 21 by

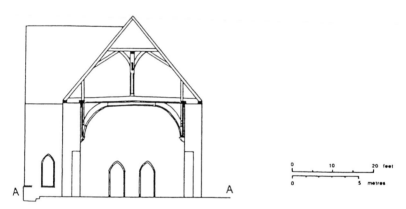

85.   East Meon, Hants: sections of hall and service wing of bishop's manor house (Roberts)

11 m set on the ground floor with central hearth was added at right angles to the original hall. There was a long extension to the south terminating in a kitchen. In the fifteenth century a courtyard was formed on the west side with a substantial gatehouse at the entry and a watergate to the river on the north side. The fourteenth-century hall is perhaps to be associated with a licence of 1337.

The bishop of Winchester among his numerous manors had one at East Meon, Hants. The village is best known for its fine Norman church but opposite to this a large part of the modest bishop's house survives. This has recently been the subject of a very thorough study

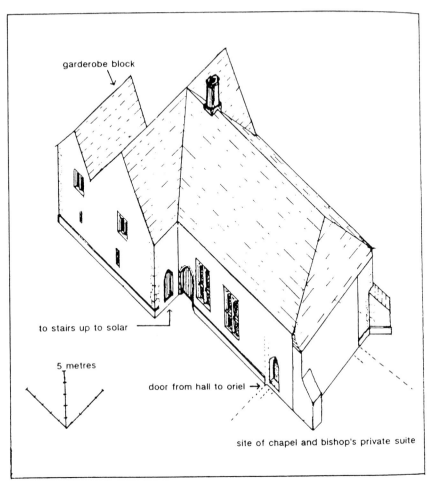

- garderobe block
- to stairs up to solar
- 5 metres
- door from hall to oriel →
- site of chapel and bishop's private suite

86.   East Meon: axonometric drawing of surviving part; the missing wing at the upper end against which it was built could have been an earlier two-storeyed hall (Roberts)

(Roberts, 1993) using the Winchester Pipe Rolls so the existing work is identified with that of 1395 by Wykeham. The ground-floor hall has tie beams in the roof supported by curved braces resting on stone corbels decorated with heads, kings on one side and bishops on the other. At the lower end there is a solar over the services (figs 85, 86). The bishop's quarter at the upper end has vanished but as the hall and solar have been added to something no longer existing the question must arise, was this T-shaped addition made to an earlier hall? We do not know, of course, but the sequence looks suspiciously like that of Tarring.

The theme of a small hall, usually on the first floor, being replaced by a larger hall, usually on the ground floor and broader, runs right through from the twelfth to the fourteenth century. It may have been required by the need to accommodate a larger number of people, the larger household, by a change of function as a courthouse or for sleeping accommodation at night. We can really only speculate. It does not feature in the fifteenth century when there was a very large number of supporting rooms. That is as far as we can take the subject.

ii   Towards a courtyard

There is very little indication in the disposition of early houses of any kind of set plan. The long ranges of the see palaces could be at right angles as at Canterbury and Durham, although in that case this may have replaced an earlier parallel arrangement. The description of the ranges as 'palaces' by Prior Laurence almost suggests he may have regarded them as independent units which would hardly require a very close arrangement. At Wolvesey and Lincoln the blocks are parallel but widely separated in time and space, at Lincoln the hall being of the later freestanding aisled type. The space between the ends being closed, a courtyard was formed more or less fortuitously.

If the abbots' houses in the west range of the cloister in figure 17 are considered, it is clear how by replacing the church with a two-storeyed chapel and the frater with a hall the plan of Old Sherborne castle was achieved. Even the dorter range on the east could be used for communal sleeping for household officials and servants. The plan at Old Sarum is cruder but evidently of the same inspiration. The modern architectural historian is fascinated by the design but contemporaries were not impressed: it seems quite unknown elsewhere. Bishops Henry and Alexander were very traditional in their plans, keeps and baileys. Farnham was no doubt a tour de force, a stone tower over the motte, but the plan otherwise is mundane. There seems to have been a hall block in the first stage and later an aisled hall, although the picture is confused.

The only other case in the twelfth century where there does seem to have been an imposed plan is Bishops Waltham (fig. 61). There the rectangular moat with its attendant buildings is thought by Hare

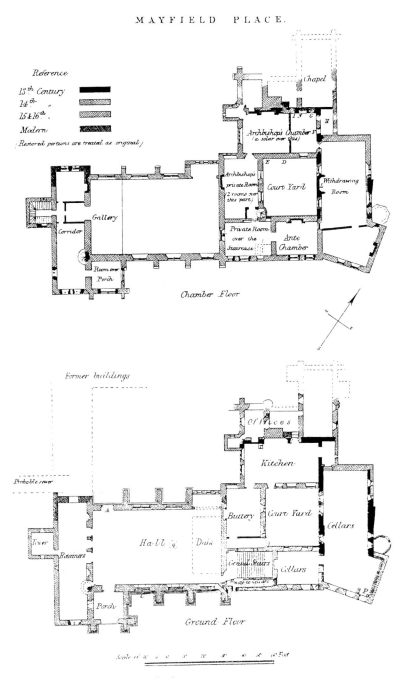

87.   Mayfield, Sussex: plan before conversion

Great Hall,
Mayfield Palace Sussex.

88.   Mayfield: the hall in 1758

(1987, 1988) to be a creation of Henry Blois after the slighting by Henry II, the earlier castle having been demolished. Perhaps this was less offensive than aggressive mottes. It created a courtyard or two courtyards although the chapel in the middle hardly suggests a very coherent plan.

This lack of interest is even more evident in the see palaces of the thirteenth century: the dog-leg pattern of Wells is forever impressed on one's memory. Nor is there much evidence to support a craving for courtyards at Hereford, Exeter, Worcester or Salisbury (especially with Bishop Poore's 'solar' reinterpreted as a hall). At Durham, Anthony Bek's fine chamber block with vaulted undercroft at right angles to the aisled hall attributed to Puiset may have created a courtyard although unfortunately the other buildings have vanished. Bek had a licence to crenellate a decidedly rectangular castle at Somerton, Lincs, in 1283 three years before his election to the see. At Lichfield, Langton put his new buildings castle-wise in a straight row against the fortified close wall (p. 60).

89.   Mayfield: inside of the hall after restoration

In the twelfth and thirteenth centuries interest had centred on the see palaces but the constriction of the close made wholesale redevelopment virtually impossible. Furthermore, by now for most sees the more permanent residence and offices were established in one or

90.   Mayfield: the outside today after conversion to chapel by Pugin
(A.E. Thompson)

two nearby manor houses. So in the fourteenth and fifteenth centuries the architectural interest moves out to the manors. The problem is that a far lower proportion survives, a handful out of two hundred or so that must have existed. For many, ground plans could be recovered by excavation, as was done at Sonning, and where parts are incorporated into later buildings much might be discovered at the time of demolition or alteration.

Another point to be borne in mind is that bishops' houses in the middle ages followed the practices of secular lords and particularly the king and cannot be regarded as developing on their own. This is not to say that they lagged behind but that the development of their secular buildings kept closely in step with the general development of lay architecture.

The archbishop of Canterbury's house at Charing, Kent, just by the parish church clearly shows courtyard tendencies: three groups of buildings of c.1300 in a very dilapidated state in a modern farmyard created two courtyards and have indeed a curiously realistic feel, especially by the gateway (fig. 71).

Of slightly later date is the well-known hall at Mayfield, Sussex, with three huge stone arches supporting the roof (figs 87 to 90). The

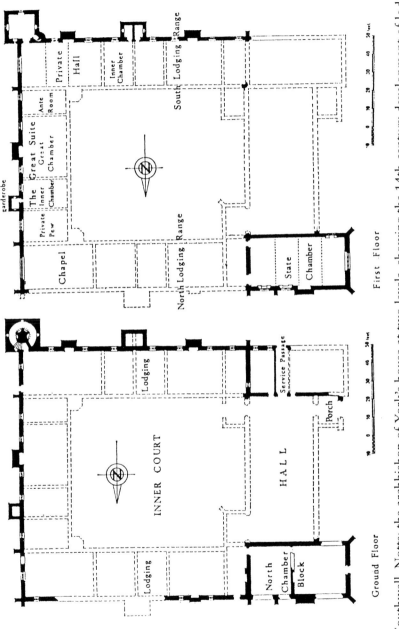

The Great Suite

garderobe

Chapel

Private Pew

Inner Chamber

Great Chamber

Ante Room

Private

Hall

Inner Chamber

North Lodging Range

South Lodging Range

State Chamber

First Floor

INNER COURT

Lodging

Lodging

Service Passage

Porch

North Chamber Block

HALL

Ground Floor

91. Southwell, Notts: the archbishop of York's house at two levels, showing the 14th-century development of lodgings and courtyard plan (Faulkner)

GROUND FLOOR

92.   Croydon: plan of archbishop's palace as it is now. Note the great development at upper end of hall engulfing the undercroft of the early hall (Faulkner)

only parallel is the stone arches supporting the roof of the hall at Conwy castle in north Wales. The arches were even more exposed in the last century before the building was restored by Pugin to serve as a chapel for a nunnery.

Two somewhat fragmentary bishops' houses must be mentioned: Southwell, a house of the archbishop of York in Nottinghamshire and Howden, a house of the bishop of Durham in the former East Riding. In the case of Southwell the plan has been worked out by Faulkner (1970) from the outer wall since nearly all the buildings have vanished including the hall (fig. 91). From this, wings extended backwards in two two-storeyed ranges of cellular lodgings of a type discussed on page 140. If they are really as early as Thoresby (1353–73) they could be one of the earliest examples.

At Howden, Bilson originally worked out the plan and Emery has also studied it (Bilson, 1915; Emery, 1996). The adjoining church required provision of a row of prebends' houses. The hall is identifi-

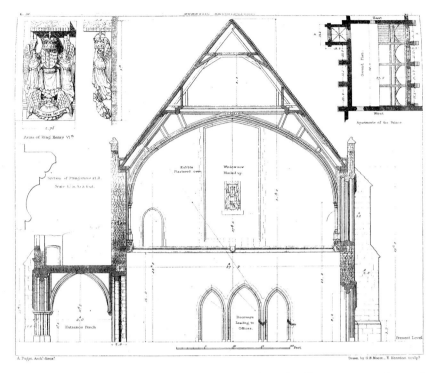

93.   Croydon: Pugin's section through porch and gallery over service end
of hall

able but the peculiarity of the courtyard arrangement is that the
buildings extend back from the wall, not vice versa. The layout is
attributed to Bishop Skirlaw (1388–1406). There are no cellular
lodgings, which gives it a more primitive look than Southwell.

The importance of the lodging ranges in the creation of the courtyard plan cannot be exaggerated (figs 92 to 95). Although the
accretions particularly at the upper end of the hall became large
they were not sufficient to form a courtyard as is well illustrated by
Faulkner's study of Croydon (Faulkner, 1970). The large group of
buildings there which included the twelfth-century hall over its
vault, known as the guardroom, and a sort of lightwell courtyard,
was transformed in the fifteenth century by the addition of lodging
ranges thrown out on either side and closed by barns and a gateway.
The lodging ranges could of course be merely put against the inside
of a castle curtain as at Amberley, Sussex, after the licence. At
Bishops Waltham they simply fill up the north side along the exist-

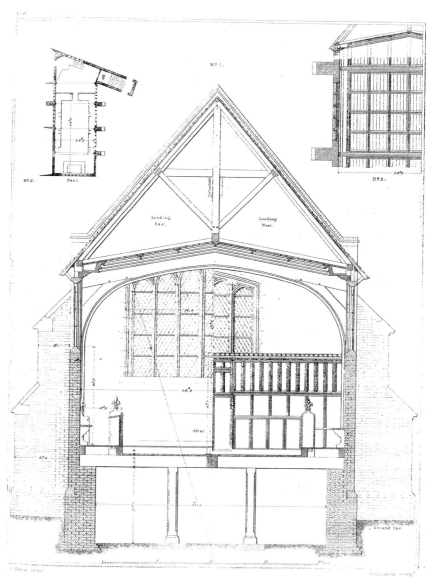

94.   Croydon: Pugin's double section of chapel, looking west on right and east on left. Note ground floor

ing moat (fig. 61). They are attributed to Cardinal Beaufort and from the Winchester Pipe Rolls have been dated 1438–42 (Hare, 1987). They are of interest as being timber-framed and a small part surviving has allowed detailed study. The rooms on the first floor

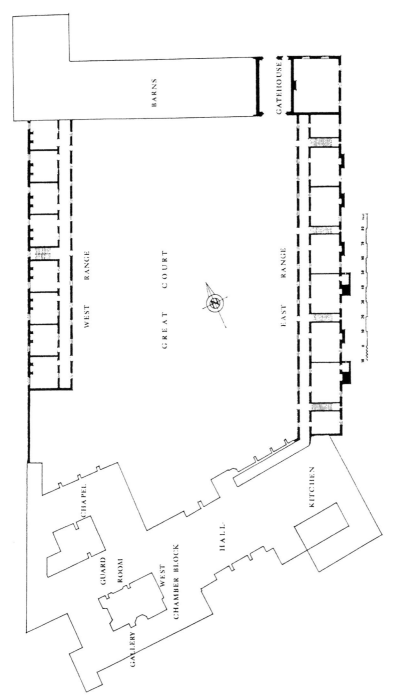

95. Croydon: Faulkner's reconstruction of the courtyard created by lodging ranges in the 15th century

141

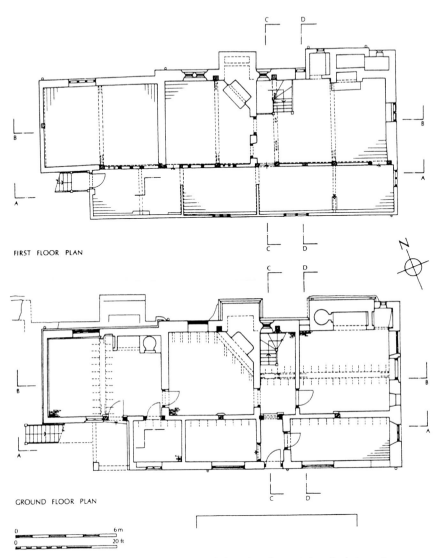

FIRST FLOOR PLAN

GROUND FLOOR PLAN

96.   Bishops Waltham: plans at both levels of surviving lodgings from long range on north side. Note gallery on inner side, individual latrines and fireplaces in external wall (Hare)

were reached by a gallery rather like the New Inn at Gloucester (fig. 96).

iii   Courtyard houses

The last hundred years before the Reformation brought disaster were something of a golden age for the construction of episcopal secular buildings in which the archbishops took the lead. Unfortunately only a fraction of the great houses survive. Knole in Kent is largely still there, much of Fulham and one court of Hampton, one range of Hatfield, and the much altered gatehouse at Esher. Of the largest at Otford, Kent, only half the outer gate and some of the range to the corner tower survive.

Two features specially characterize these courtyard houses. They have been laid out to a definite design, sometimes on a virgin site and sometimes incorporating older buildings. Even at Knole that seems to have been the case (Du Boulay, 1950). The grander ones like Hampton Court may comprise two courts. The hall is usually in the cross range facing the entry gate. More modest ones like Esher and Hatfield only had one courtyard. The second characteristic is the use of brick (except at Knole), the bricks being fired locally and there is usually a great deal of diaper decoration. Dressings were usually of stone, local craftsmen not often being skilled in the use of moulded or dressed brick.

Many of these buildings like Knole and Hampton Court are well known and often described so they need not be treated at length here. Knole has been skilfully described by that doyen of architectural analysis, Patrick Faulkner (1970). The manor was bought by Archbishop Bourgchier (1454–86) who in the course of his long episcopate erected the house. Today it consists of three courts but the outer, Green Court, is a later addition (figs 97, 98). The house is of the standard pattern, the hall lying in the cross range between the courts with the main outer gateway, flanked by two square towers outside and stair turrets inside, facing it. There is a corridor running round behind the inner face except on the hall side where there is a colonnade. The two-storeyed ranges in the main or Stone Court are timber-framed behind the façade. On the west side there were two projections for latrines, no doubt originally discharging into a moat, and the roof shows divisions for three sets of cellular lodgings. Beyond the hall and kitchen there have been many alterations although it is clear the chapel in the south-east corner is of this period. The whole of this outer court has been greatly altered.

Even with later alterations it is evident that Knole as erected by Bourgchier was a highly sophisticated building, not intrinsically

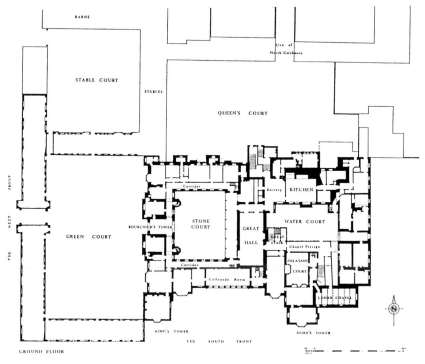

97. Knole, Kent: plan of Archbishop Bourgchier's great courtyard house. Note corridor around Stone Court. For gateway see fig. 72 (Faulkner).

different from laymen's buildings of the period, but dramatically different from earlier episcopal houses like Bishops Waltham or Croydon. The separate elements have been drawn together to make a coherent whole. Its success as a serviceable house is of course confirmed by its retention in use after the Reformation. If one is asked whether there is anything specifically episcopal about it the answer must be no, except for the chapel.

Hatfield was a convenient stopping place for the bishops of London within a day's march of the capital and saw very active use in the later middle ages. Morton, bishop of Ely 1478–86 before transfer to Canterbury, rebuilt it as a square courtyard house (fig. 99). It was replaced by the Cecil house we know today but a fine brick range of the old house was retained and used as stables (fig. 100). It was the hall range designed as one continuous structure divided internally for screens and other ancillaries with no cross wings but one roof running right through which survives. Moulded brick is

98.   Knole: aerial view from west; the front courtyard is later work

used and there are two-storeyed porches over the doorways. The late Sir Nikolaus Pevsner described it as 'one of the foremost monuments of medieval brickwork in the country' (Pevsner, *Hertfordshire*, 110).

At Esher, Surrey, Bishop Waynflete of Winchester (1447–86) erected the brick courtyard house that survived until the eighteenth century. It stood by the river Wey with surviving gatehouse, much altered by Kent, on the landward side (fig. 101).

Morton is probably to be reckoned the major building prelate of secular buildings. Apart from Hatfield and Lambeth he had authority to reconstruct all his houses in Kent, Surrey and Sussex which he certainly exercised at Maidstone, Croydon and elsewhere.[2] He set an example for the great builders of the early sixteenth century, Warham and Wolsey.

The sixteenth century opened with two further brick courtyard houses. Archbishop Warham of Canterbury (1503–32) built the great courtyard house of Otford, north of Sevenoaks near Knole, although it is not clear whether some older domestic buildings were retained. Stone dressings with brick decorated with vitrified patterns,

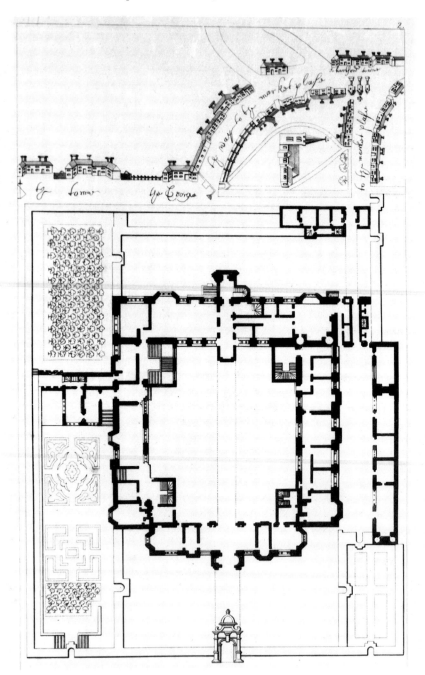

99.   Hatfield Old Palace: a 17th-century plan before the demolition of three of the ranges; only the upper one survives. Built by Bishop Morton of Ely before his transfer to Canterbury (Shaw)

100.   Hatfield: the towered porch that led into the screens passage.
Moulded brickwork throughout (without stone detail) and the surviving
roof make this a notable monument (A.E. Thompson)

diaper work, were employed, to judge by the remaining corner and
gate towers. The other brick courtyard house was that of the bishop
of London at Fulham, still occupied by the bishop, erected by
Bishop Fitzjames (1504–22). It was upriver from the city and his
cathedral of St Pauls which could easily be reached by barge. It had
been the main residence of the bishops of London since long before.
It is much less exuberant than Otford or even Hatfield must have
been, let alone Hampton Court (RCHME, *London*). The entry court
and hall survive in the standard diapered brick.
    The climax and fall of this remarkable period of episcopal build-
ing came with Thomas Wolsey, archbishop of York, 1514–30. His

THE EAST VIEW OF ESHER-PLACE, IN THE COUNTY OF SURRY.

101. Esher: gateway of Waynflete's courtyard house, much altered by Kent, is all that survives. 18th-century view by the Buck brothers

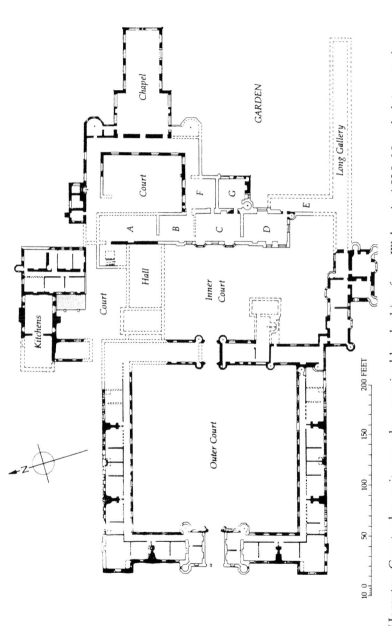

102. Hampton Court: plan as it was when acquired by the king from Wolsey in 1529. Note lodgings in first court, position of hall and chapel (Thurley)

multifarious building activities have been recently studied (Thurley, 1991). The centrepiece of Wolsey's work is Hampton Court upstream from Fulham. The whole details of his work there can be studied in the *King's Works* (*HKW*, iv (2), 216–47). It was basically a two-court design, the rear court (Clock Court) being much smaller caused by the hall in its north range not being in the usual position on the cross range (fig. 102). The large gate in the middle of this range made it impossible to put it there. Its final position, due to the king, faced the river which was the usual approach by boat. The chapel was linked to the north-east corner by a cloister. The first court, all Wolsey's work, had two levels of lodgings on three sides with back-to-back fireplaces and an internal corridor. Details will be found in the excellent guidebooks to Hampton Court.

With Hampton Court we must leave the metropolitan prelates esconced in their brick palaces waiting for the Reformation to burst over them, depriving them of so many of their palaces and reducing their status in society even if their numbers were increased by six.

iv   The surroundings of episcopal manor houses

The medieval bishop, like any landlord who occupies and operates his own property, had considerable administrative duties thrust upon him. He had a steward to look after his estates and bailiffs on the manors for their day-to-day running. However, it is clear from the rules of Grosseteste in the thirteenth century (Oschinsky, 1971) that the wise bishop familiarized himself with the workings and staff on the manors, which produced much of his income. In particular it was essential to keep an eye open for cheating: reeves, the peasants' representatives in each manor, had an evil reputation as we know from Chaucer. There was at each manor a considerable area of farmland and its appurtenances.

There were then a number of non-residential buildings, the largest of which would be the tithe barn. At Maidstone the house faces the tithe barn (? or stables) and we can appreciate its dominant position on an episcopal manor (fig. 103). The outlay incurred on just maintaining such a large building must have been considerable. At Maidstone the house faces the river on the other side, a reminder that one or more water mills were an essential part of the manor. There would also have to be buildings of various kinds for housing animals, stables, cowsheds and so on. Where security was not involved

103.   Maidstone: the archbishop's tithe barn facing the house (A.E. Thompson)

these could be further away. A building that was not only valuable for food but also symbolic of the seigneural status of the bishop was the dovecot, a round tower, its inside face covered with pigeon holes with a revolving potence in the middle for ladder access to the upper holes (Curnow and Thompson, 1969). The pigeons were bred for meat and eggs, not for racing! In the published translation of the Winchester Pipe Rolls of 1301–2 (Page, 1996) there are innumerable farming activities and appurtenances referred to.

Roberts (1986) in a recent study of the Winchester Pipe Rolls has shown the importance of fishponds in the economy of the bishops' manors, more particularly in Hampshire and Buckinghamshire, some dozen or so manors being involved. As household accounts reveal, fish, largely marine fish, were virtually a staple diet. Bred freshwater fish were probably a luxury and were supplied both to the bishop and the king. Pond fish were pike, bream, perch and roach, river fish salmon and trout. Carp breeding really only began in the fifteenth century. The great *vivaria* had been started before the pipe rolls began and Roberts attributes their creation to Henry of Blois. Surprisingly fish could be transported alive. Roberts is adamant that

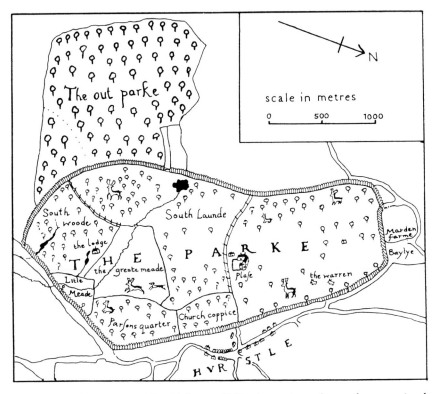

104. Merdon, Hants: The bishop of Winchester's parks as they survived in the late 16th century. The site of the castle is on the right but the bishop presumably later lived in 'Plase' (Roberts)

the breeding was not done commercially for profit but purely as a luxury food.

Every medieval seat of importance had its own deer park, an area enclosed with ditch and fence where deer could be hunted, perhaps a little artificially, primarily as a sport and only secondarily for venison. The constant maintenance of the fences was a charge on the manor and so appears in the cumulative annual accounts, the Winchester Pipe Rolls. Here again we are indebted to Roberts for an invaluable study of those in the diocese of Winchester (Roberts, 1988). He counted 23 parks, nine on the Hampshire manors. He distinguishes between enclosed parks and much larger open chases. Parks normally covered 100–200 acres but Wykeham's covered 300–1000 acres. There were three species of deer found in parks: red and roe deer which belong to the natural fauna and fallow deer brought

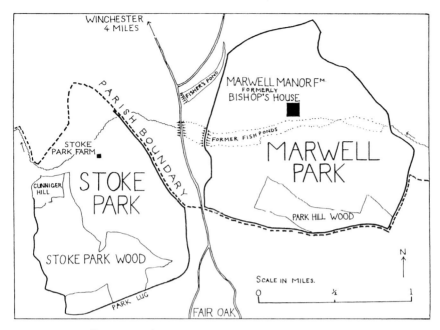

105.   Marwell, Hants: the two parks at Marwell and Stoke serving the seat of the bishop in the former (Roberts)

in by the Normans, the only breed that was bred from the four-teenth century. Much more fascinating detail is given us by Roberts and he concluded that the parks were both 'playground and larder' (figs 104, 105). The other bred wild animals, rabbits, were not extensively exploited on the Winchester manors according to Roberts, to judge by the lack of references to rabbit warrens.

Quite a different source of evidence has thrown light upon part of the surroundings of episcopal manor houses, their gardens or or-chards, by the traces left in the field. Where the ground surrounding the manor has not been built upon or ploughed up, unfortunately usually the case, traces of some kind of layout can be detected. These may take the shape of channels or moats and lines of low banks, originally forming avenues or hedges. These have been de-scribed by Christopher Taylor (1989; 1989a) at the bishop of Ely's house at Somersham, together with a valuable account of altera-tions to medieval landscape for pleasure purposes. Even more detail has been revealed at one of the archbishop of York's favourite residences, Cawood castle in Yorkshire (Blood and Taylor, 1992).

The archbishop's house stood near a loop of the river Ouse to which a canal had been dug, known as the Bishop's Dyke, to transport stone quarried from near Sherburn (Gee and Miller, 1983). Castle Garth as it is known today seems to have been an enclosed garden belonging to the house.

Traces of gardens have been detected at the bishop of Lincoln's manors at Spaldwick, Lyddington and Buckden (Taylor, 1989a). If the enhancement of surroundings by the creation of gardens was so widespread the outward appearance of episcopal manor houses must have been rather different to what one might have expected.

Notes

1. Blair, 1993. The author seems to be unaware of the duality of halls in the twelfth century or denies it, which is why his thesis fails so badly at Malmesbury. A cross wing at the upper end of the hall is virtually unknown before the thirteenth century: this thesis tries to jump the gun – it is anachronistic. Most serious is that the windows and doors on both sides of the buildings in question hardly imply that their builders were expecting one side to be engulfed by a huge, barn-like structure. The fervour of the adherents of the thesis is an act of faith, not of reason. Without evidence it can only be seen as a passing fad.
2. Entry in *DNB*.

In a vast subject like this it has not been easy to reduce it to the size of not much more than a long essay with a view to bringing out the essential features of the buildings in which we are interested. In order to make a coherent story it has been necessary to generalize, sometimes I fear rashly, and repeat points that have been made already sometimes more than once.

Nothing is known of bishops' houses in England before the Conquest, if indeed there was such a category; it would probably not be recognized in an excavation even if it were found. They are likely to have been of wood and presumably resemble other buildings of the period. On the Continent at this date a very definite type of episcopal building was in use in north Italy, derived probably from German imperial palaces. A two-storeyed rectangular block subdivided within seems to have emerged over a wide area in Germany and France (Thompson, 1995, chap. 3) by the tenth century. In France the twelfth-century bishops' palaces, although differing somewhat from north to south, clearly resemble the Italian and presumably show what was brought over at the Conquest but had not been known here before.

The appurtenances of a cathedral in Italy at this time were campanile, baptistery and the bishop's palace. After 1066 in the huge infusion of new material culture, it was not merely the new cathedral forms that were introduced into the country but also those of its chief appurtenance, the bishop's palace. At Canterbury the hall block followed very soon after the Conquest but others are a deal later, no doubt being gradually influenced by the local material culture, as seems to be the case in that curious hybrid east hall at Wolvesey. Their resemblance to the Continental hall blocks can leave no doubt as to their place of origin.

There seems to be an almost universal tendency to replace an earlier small hall with a larger new structure, retaining the earlier one for the private use of the bishop. This happened both in the see palaces and in the manors. Originally, no doubt, one simply built a hall block as at Canterbury with the main rooms over the vault but gradually this was superseded by aisled halls, barn-like and erected on the ground, a resurgence as I have suggested of the native type in a

modified form (*ibid.*, chap. 6), first at Old Sarum as the initial structure and later at Hereford. The standard hall, as I have called it,
probably emerged in the reign of Henry II, with the earliest episcopal
examples at Lincoln or Bishops Auckland. What I had not fully
understood previously was how very restricted full adoption of the
aisled hall remained: at Bishopsthorpe, Worcester, Wells and perhaps
Salisbury the thirteenth-century hall was on the first floor over a
vault; Burnell's aisled hall at Wells and Salmon's at Norwich are late
thirteenth and early fourteenth century respectively. One can see from
Emery's recent volume (1996) that the aisled hall at Bishop Auckland,
Co. Durham, is very much an odd man out in that area.

In Wales there are no aisled halls, although Peter Smith's great
book on the vernacular architecture of the principality (Smith, 1975)
shows how widespread their derivatives are in the timber-framing
areas of the north east. The retention of the first-floor hall is a fact
in the Norman or Marcher areas but not in the native Welsh ones.
In the west, Pembrokeshire, the peculiar two-storeyed house lasted
to recent times. It was not so much an ethnic difference as one based
on need: in areas of endemic warfare the first floor offered a great
deal more security than the ground floor.

This might be extended to the north of England and beyond this
even to Scotland, so far as my limited knowledge of those areas
allows; John Dunbar writes of Scottish episcopal palaces 'in general
their architecture seems to me to resemble that of the contemporary
baronial residences' (letter of 12/6/96). An exception appears to be
Kirkwall in the Orkneys which, if Simpson's (1961) redating to the
twelfth century is sound, certainly looks like the familiar hall block
(*Saalbau*) of the Continent. It could be a direct intrusion, distinctly
probable in this area.

The idea that the aisled hall is a modified native-style hall, as
suggested, seems quite compatible with evidence from bishops'
houses, which indeed reinforces it. The main cultural trait that
distinguished native from intruder was language but in the material
culture many aspects were different. In these adaptations were possible just as under Henry II they were in the familiar area of law.

In what respect do bishops' houses differ from those of lay lords?
It is difficult to say in the earlier period because so much of lay
architecture was dressed in military costume. Nevertheless Scolland's
hall at Richmond castle, Yorkshire, is surely of the same parentage
as the episcopal hall blocks. One cannot envisage a secular lord
erecting a structure like Jocelyn's hall at Wells with its internal

divisions. By the same token, apart from the absence of a domestic wing at the upper end, Burnell's hall later in the century at the same place would surely have been acceptable to king or baron. On the other hand the remarkable building, two-storeyed with a spinal arcade at Acton Burnell, Salop (West, 1981), built by the same bishop has an episcopal feel about it, perhaps deceptively (fig. 108).

If there are distinguishing features in the twelfth and thirteenth centuries they seem to be lacking in the later middle ages. The multiplication of rooms, the lodging ranges...all go hand in hand with lay architecture. Knole or Hampton Court do not differ from the contemporary secular architecture. Only the two-storeyed chapel distinguishes episcopal houses throughout the period. The capitals at Durham, the columns at Lambeth, the wooden posts at Holborn: these are the things that come to mind from bishops' houses.

Not the least interesting of bishops' houses are the castles. Three categories have been distinguished. If Gundulph's tower at Rochester is regarded as a campanile and the 'protokeep' at Wolvesey as not qualifying as a castle then only at Llandaff can we regard the castle there as of episcopal origin. Our first category is royal castles adopted by bishops near the cathedral, temporarily at Lincoln, Old Sarum and possibly Ely and permanently at Durham. At Carlisle the bishop made use of the royal castle during the Scottish incursions but was never able to regularize his position.

The second class belongs to the period of castle fever in the first half of the twelfth century, when three contiguous dioceses were involved: Salisbury, Winchester and Lincoln. Three great bishops took part: Roger of Salisbury, Henry of Winchester and Alexander of Lincoln. Roger was much older than the other two and his experiences in Wales may have set them off on this road. The primary motive was to create a new town or enhance an existing one. Eleven new castles were erected of which there are significant remains at four: Sherborne, Taunton, Farnham and Newark. Of these Sherborne with its unique claustral plan (except at Old Sarum) apparently inspired by the Benedictine cloister is in a class of its own. Otherwise the designs are fairly prosaic except for the *folie de grandeur* at Farnham, the tower rising from a freshly made motte. The whole episode is of great interest to the student of the castle, throwing light as it does on the motives for their construction and the form they took.

In the last 250 years before the Reformation, castles were not entirely abandoned and all but six of the sees maintained at least one castle in habitable condition. In the extreme south and north there was an external enemy and the reconstruction of Rose or metamorphosis of manor house into castle at Amberley, Sussex, has a self-evident explanation. Bishops now lived in a much less friendly world where crime was rampant and social stirring more evident culminating in the great storms of 1381 and 1450. There was no police force and law enforcement left a lot to be desired, so security was a do-it-yourself matter, preferably with a licence but often without. The maintenance of a single castle in the diocese provided a place of refuge, while the fortification or at least overbearing character of the bishop's house might help to overawe and disperse a mob.

Finally it may be of interest to the reader to list those bishops' houses where due to fortunate survival there are buildings of special architectural interest to demonstrate, if that be necessary, that fine buildings were erected by bishops not only in their cathedrals:

Hereford. Within the bishop's residence are the remains of an aisled hall with wooden arcades and arches of the late twelfth century. The other wooden arcades with leaf capitals associated with a bishop, but less certainly, are in the half hall at Nursestead, Kent, which has been attributed to Richard of Gravesend, bishop of London, 1280–1302 (Pryor, n.d.)

Bishop Auckland, Co. Durham. Aisled hall with marble shafts on the columns, altered into chapel with clerestorey at the Restoration, not necessarily to its detriment. The altar was put against the blocked doors at the service end. Original hall Puiset or perhaps just after 1200.

Wolvesey, Winchester. The great twelfth-century ruin with two hall blocks of different dates, originally highly ornamented, and the remarkable 'protokeep' adjoining the east hall but probably originally associated with the west hall.

Mayfield, Sussex. The archbishop's hall of mid-fourteenth century with roof supported on three great stone arches, now in a convent.

Lambeth palace. The finest feature is the splendid undercroft with marble piers and simple quadripartite vaulting. Juxon's Restoration reconstruction of the hall, and fine roof over the 'guardroom'.

Wells, Somerset. In many ways the finest palace and open to public. Jocelyn's hall, Burnell's hall, chapel and Bekington's buildings, moat and gatehouse.

St Davids, Pembrokeshire. The late thirteenth-century hall or Henry of Gower's earlier hall, if we follow Evans, and his larger, later one. All buildings raised on transverse vaults. Enhanced by setting.

106.   Durham castle: the highly decorated Norman door in the north
range attributed to Puiset (Leyland)

Sherborne (Castleton), Dorset. Bishop Roger's remarkable castle
based on Benedictine cloister, surely unique in England, if we dis-
count Old Sarum, and probably in Europe.

107.   Durham castle: the Norman wall arcading on the first floor of the
north range. Cf. Angers (Leyland)

Durham castle. The two hall blocks at right angles with the northern one containing Puiset's doorway and the arcading at dado level
on the first floor (figs 106, 107). Much later work of interest.

ACTON BURNELL SHROPSHIRE

THE HALL, WITH THE NORTH-EAST AND NORTH-WEST TOWERS.

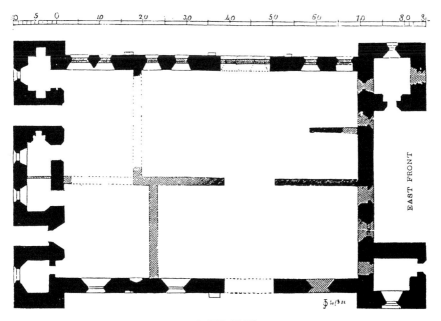

GROUND PLAN

108.   Acton Burnell, Shropshire: a 19-century plan showing central division supporting central arcade in first-floor hall, perhaps a misunderstood imitation of a Continental hall, and view as seen then (Parker)

Farnham castle, Surrey. Motte and bailey. Encased motte with base of Blois's *folie de grandeur* on top. Wooden capital in cupboard from the second hall, chapel, much Restoration work and of course the great brick tower of Waynflete, 1470–75, dominating the town.
Knole, Kent. Archbishop Bourgchier's double courtyard house.
Hatfield, Herts. The hall range of Bishop Morton's courtyard house with original roof.
Buckden, Hunts. The great brick tower and brick gatehouse of bishops Rotherham and Russel.
Hampton Court. Wolsey's work in outer court.
Acton Burnell, Shropshire. Bishop Burnell of Bath and Wells' puzzling house with its spinal division in Continental style (fig. 108).

The list could be expanded but clearly demonstrates that even with the very limited survival of bishops' palaces there remains much to see of great interest architecturally and socially.

A survey of the archbishop's palace at Canterbury in 1647

Among the surveys of episcopal property ordered by Parliament to be made when the bishops had been abolished and their property seized is one for the archiepiscopal palace at Canterbury. A copy of this exists at Lambeth Palace Library at *Comm. xiia/22, 650–59* which has been used here with the kind permission of the Trustees of Lambeth Palace Library.

Archbishop William Laud had been executed in January 1645, this survey being made nearly thirty months later in June 1647. It was done on the orders of Parliament for in spite of the Library reference Comm.(onwealth) King Charles I was still alive and in theory still ruling. All the rights of the archbishop back to ten years before the 'present Parliament', that is 1630, were to be recorded.

In fact it is clear that the surveyors were expected to give guidance on how the buildings were to be treated. Their proposals are clear: the main palace buildings to the south were to be pulled down and the materials sold. A very substantial sum of £1390 was expected to be raised. The surveyors overlooked the considerable cost of dismantling the buildings using craftsmen. Lead was far and away the most valuable item and it will be noticed how careful the surveyors were to draw attention to the lead roofs on various buildings as they went round. The materials are listed in order more or less of value, lead followed by timber and so on.

On the other hand the service buildings to the north would not have yielded a large sum on demolition and there the surveyors recommended letting at £35 per annum. The surveyors make no reference to decay and dilapidation so it is evident that most of the buildings were in good condition and indeed the surveyors say so. The recommendations were based purely on the likely financial return. So far as we can tell, what was proposed was largely carried out.

For the student of bishops' houses the survey gives us a remarkable picture of the palace and the whole range of supporting service structures required when it was in active use. This type of survey can rarely be followed in detail but the broad picture is clear. The starting point is the great thirteenth-century aisled hall; the palace buildings to the south follow. The number of vaulted ground-floor rooms is a reminder of how much of Lanfranc's building had been incorporated into later work. I fear that it cannot be assumed that either the 'Duke's hall' or 'another large hall' go back to that period! The survey should of course be compared with the excavation results in fig. 18. There must have been much later medieval and post-medieval work there: the 80-foot long wainscotted gallery or indeed the bowling green do not sound very medieval.

The 'bays' referred to in the survey are the transverse divisions of an aisled building created between the pairs of piers in the arcade, so a building could be described as of two, three, four or six bays. It was used primarily for churches but here for secular buildings. In other respects there are hardly any terms that will not be familiar to the modern reader. The surveyors constantly work by compass direction and so if it is remembered that the great hall lay east/west it will help the reader to keep oriented.

The original spelling has been retained but capitals have been economically used and new punctuation and paragraphs have been introduced. A few lines are omitted from the opening paragraph and all the later part from page 657 on dealing with claims on the property.

> A true and perfect survey of the late archbishopps pallace of Canterburie taken bye Jeffrey Sandwell, John Griffith and William Bellgrave Gent. att the aforesaid pallace the five and twentyeth daie of June Anno Domini 1647. And of all woods, rents, reversions...................courts leete and courts baron, and other possessions and hereditaments whatsoever within and every heir appertaining of what nature or quality soever having been to the said pallace belongeinge, which now are or at any time within tenn yeares before the beginnings of this present Parliament were belongeing to William Laude, late Archbishoppe of Canterburie, which here had in right of his said archbishoppricke.
>
> *In primis* the scite of the said pallace containeinge one greate hall in length one hundred sixtie eight foote, and breadth sixtie foure and in height fourtie ffote, built of stone, the rofe flatt and leaded, and supporters with two ranges of pillars. South of the east end of which greate hall adioynith a fayre passage with a small roome with a chimney and two other rooms. South beyond the same, in whiche passage is the stayrecase and stayres leading into nyne fayre chambers or studies, and further leads

into a court at the east side whereof is a buildinge usuallie called the 'Duke's hall' within and one fayre roome entringe thereunto, and are vaulted under with divers roomes for necessarie uses.

South of the foresaid Duke's hall adioynith five other roomes reacheinge to the cathedrall church. West whereof adioynith the Archbishopps Chappell in length sixtie foote and in breadth twentie foure. Out of which chappell a fayre passage with a large stayrecase descending into the cloyster belongeinge to the cathedrall. All which passages are covered with leade. West whereof another fayre passage betwyxt the dyneinge roome beinge fourtie foote longe and thirtie broade, covered with tyle. And other roomes with a gallery adioyninge north of the said dyneinge roome extendinge to the foresaid greate hall containeinge in length foure score foote and in breadthe fourteene, wainscotted. South of the said dyneinge roome is a fayre passage leadinge into another dyninge roome, west whereof another large hall. At the east end of the last-mentioned dyninge roome a small chapell covered with leade and a payre of stayres descendeinge to the said cathedrall cloysters. Southward betwixt the dyneinge room and hall first mentioned is another buildinge containeinge five roomes, covered with leade. West of the said hall two butteries and a large chamber over them, south whereof a court now used part for a garden and parte for a woodyard.

And at the north side of the skreene of the saide hall a large stayrecase covered with leade descendinge into the garden lyinge behind it and the greate hall. Westwards of the butteries aforesaid three upper roomes with another payre of stayres descending into severall usefull roomes and with two kitchins, a larder and three other necessarie roomes adioynenge.

East of the said greate hall eight roomes covered with tyle, next which east two other roomes. North whereof a fayre passage and stayrecase ascandinge [to] a hall called the Court hall containenge foure bayes where the archbishopps courts of Common lawe for the archbishopps liberty are or were usuallie kept. All which buildings are built with stone most part vaulted under for sellarage storage of wood and other necessarie supplies and uses and are covered parte with leade and parte with tyle as aforesaid, and in reasonable repayre.

The materialls of all whiche buildings being pulled downe, vizl. [videlicet] the leade, tymber, boards, iron, glasse, wainscott, stone, tyles and bricks are worthe to be solde one thousand three hundred and nynety pounds.

And parte of whiche foresaid buildings are by the house-keeper lett for the yearely rente of six pounds sixteene shillings and eight pence per annum.

Item: at the north side of the west end of the foresaid greate hall a seller with two small roomes over. North whereof a brewehouse, east of whiche brewehouse a small court or yard walled with a stone wall about twelve foote highe. Northe of the saide Brewehouse a larder and bakehouse with lodgeinge roomes over them and northe of the said bakehouse, a small kitchin with small garden east thereof. Northe of the said kitchin a small butterie and passage to a little hall, a parlour adioyninge east. Over all the foresaid lowe roomes are nyne lodgeinge chambers withe a small garrett over. Northe of the little hall one gate and passage into the pillarie. Northe of the gatehouse the porters lodge.

From thence northe six bayes of stabling all floared over and boarded. East of the saide stables a slaughter house containeinge two bayes. All which buildings northe from the greate hall are built with bricks and tyles and in good repayre. Eastwards of the said slaughter house two tenements containeinge five bayes built parte bricke parte tymber and stone slivers with tyle. Eastwards of the saide tenements one barne and bakehouse containeinge six bayes with one upper roome over the said bakehouse built with stone and sliveres with tyle. South whereof a small garden extendinge to the Court hall. All which last-mentioned buildings are in good repayre, and worthe per annum thirty five pounds.

Item: uppon the north side of the foresaid greate hall amidst the foresaid buildings lyeth one plott of ground used for a bowlenge greene, which plott with other gardens and place where the foresaide mansion or palace standeth doe containe two acres two roods, which att foure pounds per acre is worthe per annum tenn pounds.

Appendix 2
Episcopal licences to crenellate

Date	Enrolment	Bishopric	Place licensed
1200	*Rot. Chart.* 1, 60b	Coventry	Eccleshall castle (restraining interference with enclosing castle)
1257	CPR 607	Winchester	Isle of Portland, strengthen and crenellate like a castle
1271	CPR 580	Worcester	Withington, Shrop. & house in close
1272	CPR 632	York	Cawood castle, WR, Yorks
1276	CPR 140	Ely	Fen Ditton, Cambs
1284	CPR 110	(B. & Wells)	Acton Burnell, Shrop.
1285	CPR 150	(St Davids)	Pleasley, Derbys
1286	CPR 220	B. & Wells	Close for better security
1290	CPR 393	Exeter	See palace
1291	CPR 451	(York)	Little Compton, Glos (now Warwicks)
1299	CPR 409	C. & Lichfield	Close at Lichfield (houses in)
1301	CPR 561	C. & Lichfield	Thorpe Waterville, Northants,
1305	CPR 367	"	London, house by Temple Bar
1306	CPR 462	"	Beaudesert, Warwicks & Ashby, Northants and all episcopal palaces in England
1316	CPR 436	Lincoln	Close, dean and chapter, 12 ft wall
1318	CPR 257	"	Close, raise wall and add turrets
1322	CPR 140	Exeter	See palace and close
1327	CPR 159	Salisbury	Close – dean & chapter
1328	C. Chart 82	"	City – bishop, canons, citizens
1328	Turner & Parker 111, 422	Norwich	See palace & all manors of bishopric
1329	CPR 453–4	Lincoln	See palace
1336	CPR 245	Carlisle	La Rose castle, Cumb.
1336	CPR 30	Lincoln	Nettleham & Stow, Lincs & Lyddington, Rutland
1337	CPR 498	Salisbury	Salisbury (bishop's manor), Bishop's Cannings, Ramsbury, Potterne, Bishop's Woodford in Wilts, Sonning in Berks & Sherborne in Dorset, Chardstock in Devon and house in Fleet Street
1340	CPR 465	B. & Wells	Wells see palace
1346	CPR 61	London	Bishops Stortford castle, Herts
1348	CPR 438	C. & Lichfield	Close – bishop, dean and chapter
1355	CPR 252	Carlisle	La Rose castle, Cumb.
1359	CPR 290	Salisbury	Edington Hospital, Wilts: rector, brethren and bishop

Date	Enrolment	Bishopric	Place licensed
1377	CPR 9	Salisbury	City, see palace and the 8 manors in the licence of 1337
1337	CPR 76	Chichester	Amberley castle, Sussex
1379	CPR 377	Exeter	Chudleigh, Devon or elsewhere, to make a fortalice
1383	CPR 333	York	Rest Park, Yorks, to erect a fortlet
1387	CPR 381	Norwich	N. Elmham & Gaywood, Norfolk
1397	CPR	(Carlisle)	Penrith, Strickland elected bishop 1399
1426	CPR 351	(Winchester, Durham et al.)	The Moor, Rickmansworth – shared licence
1447	C. Chart. R. 94–5	Chichester	Sussex manors as follows: Aldingbourne, Amberley, Bexhill, Broyle, Cakeham, Drungeswick, Ferring, Preston, Selsey, Sidlisham, Turzes & W. Wittering
1451	CPR 473	B. & Wells	See palace, Wells, as in 1340
1474	C. Chart. R.	Durham	Bridgecourt in Battersea and impark
1523	L. & P. iii no. 3146	C. & Lichfield	Close – licence to Dean Denton, as 1299 & 1348

The dioceses are arranged alphabetically including the Welsh dioceses. They all fell within the provinces of Canterbury and York (only Galloway is omitted from the latter). Within each diocese the houses are arranged in the order: see palace, London house, manor castles, manor houses. Only manors in which there is reason to believe there was a house of episcopal standard are included; although only a working list it is hoped that there are no serious omissions. An asterisk implies frequent use indicated by a register. The old counties are used for location.

Bangor

See palace: NW of cathedral, stone facing over timber framing, projecting wings, W half c. 1500. Now town hall (RCAHMW, *Carn.*, 2, 9–10, fig. 19)
London house: B. Benedict (1408–17) dated many documents there (Pryce, 1922). Schofield, no. 151, Shoe Lane, Holborn. Gift in 1280
Manor houses: Caernarfon, 'in hospicio suo' (Pryce, 1922)
Edern? (*Valor*)
Gogarth, near Llandudno. Low walls, hall 15 by 9 m, 5 rooms; 'and ther be the ruines of a place of the bishops of Bangor' (RCAHMW, *Carn.*, 3, 112–3; Leland, 13, 53)
Llanallgo, Anglesey? (Pryce, 1922)
Treffos, Anglesey (*Valor*)? Newborough

Bath and Wells

See palace at Bath: SW of cathedral, earlier hall covered by later one identified in excavation (Chapman, Davenport and Holland, 1995)
See palace at Wells: 'castelle lyke' (Leland, 1, 146). Still in use. Moated enclosure with buildings of B. Jocelin, Burnell and Bekington in irregular disposition with gatehouse (Parker, 1863)

London house: Bath inn, Bath or Hampton Place nr St Clement's Danes outside Temple Bar (Stow, 489b). Very prominent in Wyngaerde's view. Schofield, no. 157, Strand (Kingsford, 1922; Schofield, 1995)

Manor castles: none?

Manor houses: Acton Burnell, Shropshire (not diocesan). Licence 1284. Two-storeyed block with spinal arcade and corner turrets of unique form (Salmon n.d.; Radford 1961; West, 1981)

*Banwell, Som. Chapel and fragments in Banwell Court (Pevsner)

*Blackford, Som. (Rendell, 1963)

Cheddar, Som. Rahtz's excavation revealed small hall with transverse wings (1979)

*Chew Magna, Som. Perhaps on site of Chew Court

*Claverton, Som.

*Dogmersfield, Hants. Park in deserted village survives (Meirion-Jones, 1969)

Evercreech, Som. 'now yn ruine' (Leland, 1, 294)

Pucklechurch, Glos. 'a parke and a goodly lordshipe' (Leland, 5, 102)

*Wiveliscombe, Som. Erected by B. Drakensford (1309–29). Only a gateway survives (Pevsner)

Wookey, Som. Moated area SW of church (Hasler and Luker, 1994)

Wyke, Glos. (? Wyck Rissington)

Canterbury

See palace: Lanfranc's palace due W of cloister, L-shaped after extension, a large aisled hall of 8 bays added c. 1200 with ancillaries, the W Porch and fragments survive on N side. Excavations by Rady, Tatton-Brown and Bowen (1991)

London house: Lambeth palace on Surrey side of Thames from early 13th century. 15th-century gate tower, 13th-century chapel, and hall reconstructed at Restoration (RCHME, *London*, 2, 79–86)

Manor castles: *Saltwood castle, Kent. Enfeoffed in earlier period but actively occupied and rebuilt by Ab. Courtenay in late 14th century who erected great residential gate tower, two-storeyed chapel and great chamber over vault (Hussey, 1942; sequence with plans in Emery, 1994)

Tonbridge castle, Kent. Always held by feoffees

Manor houses: *Aldington, Kent

Bersted, Sussex

*Bishopsbourne, Kent

Burstow, Surrey

*Charing, Kent. Extensive remains among farm buildings with impressive hall of c. 1300 on E side of irregular courtyard (Kipps, 1934; Newman in Pevsner, 252–3)

*Chartham, Kent

*Croydon, Surrey. Late medieval courtyard house with lodgings of which the hall with complex around two courtyards survives (Anderson, 1882, chap. 9; Faulkner, 1970, 133–5)

Ford, Kent. Demolished 1650. Unpublished excavations have revealed foundations (oral report)

Gillingham, Kent

Harrow, Middx

Hayes, Middx. (Southern, 1962, 67)

Knole, Kent. Site acquired by Ab. Bourchier in 15th century who created great two-courtyard house that survives with later additions (Faulkner, 1970; Newman in Pevsner, 342–9)

Langley Marish, Bucks

*Lyminge, Kent

Maidstone, Kent. Considerable remains of late 14th-century palace behind an Elizabethan frontage. Worked out by Rigold (1969)

*Mayfield, Sussex. Mid 14th-century hall divided by three great stone arches into four bays (restored by Pugin) and 13th-century buildings (Roberts, 1867)

*Mortlake, Surrey. Nothing survives (*VCH*, 4, 69–70; Bosanquet, 1964, 73, 210)

Northfleet, Kent

Otford, Kent. Rebuilt by Ab. Warham, 1503–18, two courtyards in brick with stone dressings, octagonal tower, cloister. Ruins visible (Hesketh, 1915; C. P. Wood, 1975; Newman in Pevsner, 428–9)

Pagham, Sussex (Bosanquet, 1964, 211)

*Pinner, Middx. Headstone Manor. Rectangular brick-lined moat enclosing in corner service wing and first bay of 4-bay (excavated) hall, aisle posts, tie beam, crown post, probably attributable to Archbishop Stratford (1333–48). Much later expansion. Ten-bay 16th-century tithe barn (RCHME, *Middx*, 102–3; *TLMAS*, 1870, 3, 185; Cherry in Pevsner, *London*, 3 (1991), 280–1; *The Times*, 27 September, 1997)

*Slindon, Sussex. Stump of tower of medieval house survives (Nairn in Pevsner)

*Teynham, Sussex
West Tarring, Sussex. Solar on undercroft (probably original hall), early 13th century with ground-floor hall of c. 1300 built on to it, complete with two-storeyed lower end (Packham, 1923)
*Wingham, Kent. Associated with college
Wrotham, Kent. Abandoned in favour of Maidstone in 14th century (Du Boulay, 1966, 239)

Carlisle

See palace: apparently none but had houses in Carlisle in later middle ages
London house: Carlisle house in Strand with garden extending to Thames and separated from Durham house by lane (Wilson, 1912, 16; Schofield, 158)
Manor castles: *Bewley, Westm. Rectangular building survives with hall 6 by 12 m on first floor with separate chamber at end and a tower at the SE corner (RCHME, 43–4)
Linstock, Cumb. Towerhouse with attached building (Wilson, 1912)
Penrith, Cumb. Licences to William Strickland in 1397 and 1399 who became B. of Carlisle in 1399 when he lost the castle to the Nevilles (Emery, 1996, 1, 237–9)
*The Rose, Cumb. Licences 1336 and 1355. Quadrangular inner ward with outer curtain but much later alteration. Still occupied by bishop (Emery, 1996, 1, 244–6)
Manor houses: *Horncastle, Lincs
*Melbourne, Derbyshire

Chichester

See palace: SW of cathedral, largely medieval: square kitchen, early 13th-century chapel and infilled hall to W (Hannah, 1909; VCH, 3, 147–53
London house: land by New Temple given by Henry III upon which a 'noble house' erected, now occupied by Lincoln's Inn. Schofield no. 47. Present hall built 1489–92 when on long lease to Society of Apprentices in Law
Manor castle: *Amberley, Sussex, an ordinary manor house converted to castle, licence of 1377, repeated 1447. Original hall of c.

1200 and late 14th-century hall, three lower end doors. Substantial curtain with gatehouse (Peckam, 1921)
*Aldingbourne, 1447 (*VCH*, 4, 134)
Bexhill, 1447, general plan and parts of fabric survive in manor house
Bishopstone
Broyle, 1447
*Cakeham, W Wittering, 1447, part of vaulted undercroft of hall (15 by 7 m) c. 1200 and early 16th-century brick tower (*VCH*, 4, 217–8; Nairn in Pevsner, 377–8)
*Drungeswick, Loxwood, 1447
Ferring, 1447
Preston, 1447
Selsey, 1447, traces in Manor farm?
Turzes, 1447

Coventry and Lichfield

[Chester: from the brief period as centre of see after 1075 there is said to have been a palace at St John's church]
Coventry: single block survived NE of St Michael's church in 1224–5 until last century (Lilley, 1994). According to Leland (2, 108) the bishop 'hathe an old palace in Coventrie'
Lichfield: licences 1299 and 1348 to fortify the close. Plan of Langton's palace in 1685 exists before demolition. Large hall with vaulted undercroft whose width suggests possible spinal arcade, chapel perhaps moved from N to S (*VCH*, 14, 63; Tringham, 1993)
London house: in Strand by Strand bridge built by B. Langton on licence of 1305 (Stow, 490)
Manor castle: *Eccleshall, Staffs. Licence mentioned in letter re-straining interference with enclosure of Brewood and the castle. Rebuilt by B. Langton and plans of 1687 which survive show a rectangular two-storeyed block with hall over vaulted undercroft (*VCH*, 1, 370; Maddison, 1993)
Castle Ashby, Northants? Licence to Langton 1306. Leland de-scribes it as 'clene down' (1, 7) before Elizabethan rebuilding
Manor houses: Beaudesert, Staffs. Licence 1306
Bishops Itchington, Warwicks
Bishops Tachbrook, Warwicks
Brewood, Staffs

Cannock, Staffs
Farndon, Cheshire
*Heywood, Staffs. According to Leland properly called Shugborough (2, 109)
Langton, Staffs
*Prees, Salop
Rugeley, Staffs
*Sawley, Derbyshire
*Tarvin, Cheshire
Thorpe Waterville, Northants. Licence 1301. Farmhouse with lancets and kingpost roof (Pevsner, 429)
Wybunbury, Cheshire

Durham

See palace: started as Conqueror's royal castle but from 1070s served as bishop's palace. Motte crowned with shell keep and bailey with two ranges at first parallel but E one moved N to form curtain. Famous for Puiset's doorway and wall arcade. 11th-century chapel (*VCH*, 3, 64–91; Leyland, 1994; Thompson, 1994)
London house: Durham house built by B. Hatfield (1345–81) in Westminster at Charing Cross, by riverside. View of hall in Wyngaerde (Colvin and Foster, 1996, Dr. 1). Schofield, no. 161. Licence in 1474 to build house with towers and impark in Battersea on S side of river
Manor castles: Barnard castle, Durh., bishops' claims rarely bore fruit (Saunders, 1971, 2–3)
Bishop Middleham, Durh. Abandoned in 15th century (*VCH*, 3, 204)
*Crayke castle, NR, Yorks. On site of early monastery consists of two 15th-century blocks, perhaps containing halls (Adams, 1990; Emery, 1996, 1, 327–9)
Norham castle, Northumb. Keep starting as two-storeyed hall under B. Flambard completed by Puiset and 12th-century curtain with alterations. Castle on Scottish border (Hunter Blair and Honeyman, 1966; Dixon and Marshall, 1993)
*Northallerton, NR, Yorks. Two 12th-century earthworks exist. According to Leland the one retained in use was well moated and strong (*VCH, Yorks.*, 215; *Yorks, NR*, 422)

[Somerton, Lincs. Licence 1281 to Anthony Bek to build square castle with corner towers; B. of Durham 1283–1311]

Stockton on Tees, Durh. A survey of 1577 describes buildings, massive curtain and towers so evidently qualifies as castle (Raine, 1876; *VCH*, 3, 353–4)

Tweedmouth, Northumb. According to Brown (1959, 274) built by Philip of Poitou, then B. of Durham before 1208 and demolished 1209

Manor houses: *Bishop Auckland, Durh., the main residence of the bishopric through the middle ages and up to the present day. Splendid four-bay aisled hall of c. 1200 (Puiset?) and two-storeyed block of Bek a hundred years later. Two-storeyed chapel demolished by Parliament after Civil War (Leland, 1, 70; Raine, 1852; Hodgson, 1896; Emery, 1, 51–3)

*Darlington, Durh. The B. of Durham 'hath a praty palace in this toune' (Leland, 1, 69)

Easington, Durh. (Emery, 1, 52–3, 55–7)

Evenwood, Durh.

*Howden, ER, Yorks: SE of church, irregular courtyard with gateway facing hall of which very little survives. Built by B. Skirlaw (1388–1406). Plan worked out by Bilson (1913) and more detail in Emery (1996, 353–6)

*Riccall, ER, Yorks, nr Selby. House called Wheel Hall

[Rickmansworth, Herts. The More. Shared interest with B. of Winchester and others. licence 1426 (*VCH*, 2, 375; Biddle, Barfield and Millard, 1959)]

Walsingham, Durh. (Emery, 1, 52–3)

Ely

See palace: Cherry Hill, the motte and bailey adjoining the priory, possibly royal originally and abandoned in 12th century (Brown, 1959). B. Hugh of Northwold (1229–45) probably built *aula episcopalis* SW of cathedral that grew into a courtyard. Only the brick flanking towers of B. Alcock survive today (*VCH*, 4, 82–3 with plan; Hussey, 1928)

London house: Ely house in Holborn, site given by John Kirkby (1286–90) but built by B. Thomas Arundel in 14th century. Plan made by Grose before demolition showing two-storeyed chapel on N side of a cloister with hall and ancillaries on its S side. Only the chapel survives. (Aston, 1967, 271–5). Schofield, no. 106. Part of cloister exposed 1985

Manor castle: *Wisbech, Cambs. The Conqueror built a castle here in 1072 but it had come into the hands of the bishop by the 12th century (Brown, 1959, 280). In active use throughout the middle ages, rebuilt c. 1480 but nothing survives today

Manor houses: *Balsham, Cambs
Doddington, Cambs
*Downham, Cambs. Not near church, two brick buildings of B. Alcock survive, both two-storeyed and E one with elaborate doorway. Their relationship to overall, presumably courtyard, plan uncertain
Fen Ditton, Cambs. Licence 1276. The Biggin, two-storeyed fragment of courtyard within large moat (RCHME, *NE Cambs*, 58–60)
Greet Shelford, Cambs. Moat
Hardwick, Cambs. Moats (RCHME, *W. Cambs*, 128b)
*Hatfield, Herts. The fine W range that contains hall and ancillaries is the only range of the square courtyard that survives and has two-storeyed porches and original roof. Moulded brick. Erected by B. Morton before his translation to Canterbury (RCHME, 58–61)
Little Gransden, Cambs. Possible site NE of church
Little Hadham, Herts. Hadham Hall on its site (RCHME, 145)
*Somersham, Hunts. Surrounding moats, fishponds and deer park studied to show altered landscape (Taylor, 1989; RCHME, 238–9)
Totteridge, Herts
Willington, Cambs

Exeter

See palace: parts of aisled hall built by B. Brewer (1224–44) survive, 23 by 15 m, divided into three bays by wooden arcade posts with stiff-leaf capitals, to SE of cathedral (Chanter, 1932; *Arch. J* (1990) Supp., 41–5)
London house: 'memorable for greatness on the River of Thames... who was first builder thereof I have not read but that Walter Stapleton was a great builder in the raigne of Edward the second is manifest' (Stow, 489a). After Stow the hall was built by Bishop Lacy in the reign of Henry VI. Schofield, no. 156, Strand (Essex House), acquired 1310 and hall rebuilt 1420–55
Manor castle: apparently none

Manor houses: Bishops Tawton, Devon. Early site of see
Bishopsteighton, Devon. All that survives are walls of B. Grandison's
chapel with ogee-headed lancets which probably stood on the S side
of a courtyard of which traces remain (Laithwaite, Blaycock and
Westcott, 1989)
*Chudleigh, Devon. Vaults and other fragments at Palace Farm
*Clyst Honiton, Devon, Bishop's Court. Built by B. Branescombe in
1285. Drawings by Swete show courtyard with hall range on W and
chapel on S (Brooks, 1990). Survey of barn and stable by Alcock
(1966)
Crediton, Devon. Site of see before Exeter
East Horsley, Surrey. 'a praty lytle manor place' (Leland, 5, 3)
*Farringdon, Devon. Also called Bishops Clyst
Lanner, nr St Allen, Corn.
Lawhitton, Launceston, Corn.
Paignton, Devon. 'of the palace some tall works and one tower
(much restored) remain' (Pevsner)
Pawton, Corn. Deer park
Penryn, Corn. Small building that stood adjoining park (Wingfield,
1979)
St Germans, Corn. 'And at this day the Bisshop of Exceter hathe a
place callid Cudden Beke joyning hard upon the southeast side of
the same towne' (Leland, 1, 325)

Hereford

See palace: S of cloister on S side of cathedral. 12th-century hall
famous for its wooden arcades and fragments of 11th-century two-
storeyed chapel (RCHME; Blair, 1987)
London house: unusually in City on W side of Old Fish Street at
junction with Lombard Street in Queenhithe Ward, built of stone and
timber (Webb, 1853–5, xxiv–vii). Schofield, no. 111, Lambeth Hill.
Site bought 1234 and chapel converted to St Mary Mounthalt 1346
Manor castle: Lydney North, Bishops Castle, Salop. Very close to
Welsh border. Episcopal since 12th century. Substantial earthworks
remain (Brown, 1959, under Lydbury North)
Manor houses: Bishops Frome, Heref. At Cheyney Court outbuilding perhaps chapel. Park, mill, dovecote (RCHME, 2, 11)
*Bosbury, Heref. Old Court Farm, part 15th century with moulded
ceiling and gateway with pedestrian entry (RCHME, 2, 19–20)

Bromyard, Heref.
Colwall, Heref.? Park Farm on site (RCHME, 254)
Cradley, Heref.? present parish hall (RCHME, 262)
Eastnor, Heref.?
Hampton, Bishop, Heref.
Ledbury, Heref. 'fayre mansion place' (Leland, v, 184). Perhaps the 14th-century hall house described in RCHME, 2, 113a
*Prestbury, Glos. Twin moats excavated by H. O'Neill in 1956. Early with aisled hall c. 1200
Ross-on-Wye, Heref. Ruinous according to Leland (5, 184) Cf. RCHME, 2, 164
*Stretton Sugwas, Heref. Sugwas Court on its site. 12th-century doorway in outbuilding, perhaps chapel (RCHME, 2, 177)
Upton Bishop, Heref. Upton Court is 14th-century house with original roof (RCHME, 2, 194)
Whitbourne, Heref. Whitbourne Court perhaps on its site

Lincoln

See palace: B. Remigius probably started in an annex on E side of royal castle with its own motte; B. Alexander moved out to the Roman East gate N of cathedral and later he was authorized to break through the Roman wall S of the cathedral to present site. 12th-century E hall and St Hugh's W hall with B. Alnwick's 15th-century gate tower in between. Impressive first-floor kitchen to S of W hall. Licences for close 1316 and 1318 and palace in 1329 (Faulkner, 1974; Thompson, 1998).
London house: 'Adjoyning to this old Temple was sometime the Bishop of Lincolnes Inne.. Robert de Curars[Chesney] builded it about the yeere 1147...' (Stow, 486b). Schofield, no. 102, Holborn *Manor castles*: Banbury, Oxon. B. Alexander founded castle to create borough described by Harvey in Lobel (1969). Excavations by Rodwell (1976) which showed concentric castle of two periods
Newark, Notts. Castle founded by B. Alexander probably at same time as the bridge over the Trent was built that carried the Great North Road. The intention was to enhance an existing borough; the castle remained in active use throughout middle ages. Domestic buildings lay on the inside of the river wall (Braun, 1935; Marshall and Samuels, 1997)

Sleaford, Lincs. Another of B. Alexander's projects to create a borough associated with a bridge at New Sleaford (Beresford, 1967, 466). Only mounds survive from the castle although in active use in 15th century
Manor houses: Biggleswade, Beds
Bishop Norton, Lincs
*Buckden, Hunts. Great brick tower and gateway of B. Rotherham (1472–80), B. Russell (1480–94), and foundations of earlier hall and chapel. Plan RCHME, 34–6
Cropredy, Oxon
Dorchester, Oxon. See transferred from here to Lincoln in 1070s. Leland says only foundations visible (1,118)
*Fingest, Bucks
Kilsby, Northants
Leicester. E of town
*Lyddington, Rutland. Licence 1336. Immediately adjoining the church is a 14th-century range, perhaps original hall block, fine ceiling and window glass on first floor (great chamber). Excavations by C. and P. Woodfield (1988) revealed large attached hall to N. Ponds and gardens known. In 1601 refounded by Lord Burghley as bedehouse (*VCH*, 2, 188–92; C. and P. Woodfield, 1981–1988
Louth, Lincs
*Nettleham, Lincs. 3 miles NE of Lincoln. Only mounds remain
Spaldwick, Hunts. Large enclosure near church (Taylor, 1989)
*Stow Park, Lincs. Licence 1336
Wooburn, Bucks (*VCH*, 3, 107)

Llandaff

See palace: the Bishop's Castle is separated from the cathedral by a re-entrant valley to the N (no close). Probably built by B. William de Braose (1266–87). Irregular quadrilateral with towers on the S corners and large gatehouse and two-storeyed hall forming the two northern corners. (Johns, 1974; RCAHMW, *Glamorgan*, 3, Pt. 1b, forthcoming)
London house: In the Strand adjoining church of the Nativity of Our Lady (Stow, 490)
Manor castle: –
Manor houses: Bishopston, Gower. Length of wall 15 m long and 2.5 m high with doorway and windows (? barn) (RCAHMW)

Bishopston, Mon.
Mathern, Mon: From 15th century replaced Llandaff as residence. 'Mathern is a preaty pyle in Base Venteland [Gwent] longging to the Bisshop of Landafe' (Leland, 3, 44). Tower, porch and other parts to N of John de la Zouch (1408–23) (RCAHMW). Heavily restored by Tipping (information from John Newman).

London

See palace: by the NW corner of old St Pauls and included a two-storeyed chapel as at Lambeth. '…a large thing for Receit wherein divers Kings have been lodged, and a great Household hath bene kept, as appeareth by the Great Hall, which of late yeers, since the rebatement of Bishops livings, hath not been furnished with Household Meynie and Guests, as was meant by the builders thereof…' (Stow, 412b; Simpson, 1905)
Manor castle: Bishops Stortford, Herts. Motte and bailey with stone structure on motte. Licence 1346. Ruinous in Leland's time (RCHME, 64)
Manor houses: Berdon, Essex
Broxbourne, Herts
*Fulham, Middx. In its late medieval form as built by B. Fitzjames (1506–22), a double courtyard with brick ranges with diaper decoration, squat tower over entry facing the hall. Near the Thames. Still in use following later alterations (RCHME, *W. London*, 34–6)
Harringay, Middx
Much Hadham, Herts. A brick-encased, timber-framed house of H-plan survives dating from early 16th century (RCHME, 154)
[Nursestead, Kent. Non-diocesan, remarkable survival of half a hall with wooden aisle posts with leaf capitals, probably built by Richard of Gravesend, B. of London 1280–1303. (Pryor, n. d.)]
Orsett, Essex. Earthwork enclosures with later house outside (RCHME, 4, 106)
*Stepney (Stebbenheth), Essex.? The same as the 'Bisshops House' at Bethnal Green (Leland, 4, 128)
Wickham Bishops, Essex. Wickham Hall, moated, perhaps on site (RCHME, 2, 259)

Norwich

See palace: B. Losinga's palace, 1104–6, extended northwards from the 4th bay W of the N transept. Two-storeyed hall with a broader rectangular block at its N end. A further two-storeyed late 12th-century building and chapel before the early 14th-century great six-bay aisled hall of B. Salmon, of which only the porch survives. Licence for palace 1328. S of this a mid-15th century corridor linked the palace to the cathedral N transept (Whittingham, coloured plan, 1949, 1980; Atherton et al., 1996)

London house: 'Next beyond this Durham house is another great house sometime belonging to the Bishop of Norwich and was his London lodging which now pertaneth to the Archbishop of York...' When Henry VIII took over York Place to form Whitehall the B. of Norwich lost his house to the Duke of Suffolk, later the displaced Ab. of York, and had to move S of the Thames (Stow, 495a). Schofield, no. 160, Strand

Manor castle: one of the dioceses without a castle

Manor houses: the licence of 1328 covered all the houses of the bishopric

Bacton, Suff.

*Blofield, Norf.

Eccles, Norf. The village since lost to the sea

Gaywood, Norf. Licence 1387. A survey of 1487 shows it consisted of two moated enclosures, the inner containing the domestic buildings (Bradfer-Lawrence, 1952)

*Hoxne, Suff.

North Elmham, Norf. Licence 1387. The remains thought to be those of a Saxon cathedral now regarded (not wholly convincingly) as a chapel of the Norman bishops were transformed into a fortified house by B. Despenser. The nave became an undercroft and turrets flanked the doorway (Rigold, 1963).

*South Elmham, Suff. The apsed flint building seems to be a pre-Conquest church and is unconnected with the moated site that contained the house of the bishop, partly surviving in S. Elmham hall

*Terling, Essex. Stopping place on way to London. The present manor house is 15th century (RCHME, 2, 229)

Thornage, Norf. Buttressed flint and brick two-storeyed range with new tracery blocked arches

Wykes-by-Ipswich

Rochester

See palace: the rectangular two-storeyed block constructed beyond the line of the Roman wall probably contained B. Gundulph's original first-floor hall, albeit much altered later. With ancillary ranges a regular courtyard was created to the SW of the cathedral that was demolished after the Reformation (Rye, 1887; Hope, 1900; Tatton-Brown, 1984)

London house: originally La Place behind Lambeth Palace but subsequently behind Winchester House, Southwark: 'Adjoyning to this on the South side thereof is the Bishop of Rochester's Inn or Lodging by whom first erected I doe not now remember...' (Stow, 449b: Pearman et. al., 1918). Schofield, no. 158

Manor castle: –

Manor houses: (Pearman, Tait and Thompson, 1918)

Bromley, Kent Hasted (1, opp. 91) has an engraving of the house in 1750, clearly a medieval house in origin, which was demolished in 1770

*Halling, Kent. Wall in churchyard with three blocked lancets (?chapel) (Newman in Pevsner, 301)

Stone, Kent. Stood near churchyard and according to Hasted (2, 388) 'never to have been dignified with name of palace'

*Trottiscliffe, Kent

St Asaph

See palace: the existing palace is apparently an 18th-century building but the medieval bishop may have lived at Esgobty farm to the SW, recently pulled down

London house: not identified

Manor castle: –

Manor houses: Llandegla, Denbigh (*Valor*)

Meliden, Flint (*Valor*)

St Davids

See palace: almost due W of cathedral, a courtyard with remains of buildings on three sides. The earlier hall and solar on E side on the first floor over transverse vaults with its kitchen at the S end, replaced by B. Henry of Gower's splendid first-floor hall at right angles in the 14th century, re-using the same kitchen, and with porch and chapel on N side. Decorative open arcading in chequer work below crenellations all the way round. Rose in gable wall. (Jones and Freeman, 1856; Radford, 1955; Williams, 1981; W. Evans, 1991)

London house: 'The Bishop of S. David had his Inne over-against the North side of this Bridewell...' (Stow, 436–7). This is just W of Temple Bar. Schofield, no. 37. An exposed undercroft may belong

Manor castle: Llawhaden, Pembs. Originally a ringwork, then a structure with round mural towers replaced in c. 1300 by two-storeyed rectangular structures with hall over vaulted ground floor and chamber and kitchen projecting as square towers, chapel to SW. The gatehouse was refronted later in 14th century (Radford, 1955; R. Turner, 1991)

Swansea, Glam. Leland says the old castle built by the Normans was destroyed by Llywellen the Great 'and it stoode by the bissop of S. Dauids castel that now is there' (3, 127). The decorative arcading below the crenellations is identical to that at St Davids palace. The impressive remains consist of hall and chamber set over transverse vaults and a tower (Williams, 1981; Evans, 1983)

Manor houses: Abergwili, Carm. Possibly house associated with college

Lamphey, Pembs. Three two-storeyed buildings and gateway survive: the original hall superseded to the W by a larger hall and finally the hall of Henry of Gower to the SE with the decorative arcading below the parapet (Radford, 1948: Williams, 1981; R. Turner, 1991)

Llanddew, Breck. Ruin in Vicarage garden (RCHMW)

Llandewi, Gower

Llanddywy, Cards

Pleasley, Derb. Licence 1285. Perhaps a place of retreat during Welsh wars; cf. B. of Carlisle at Melbourne

Trefine, Pembs. Presumably the same as Llanrhian of Leland (3, 65) where the bishop 'hath a place'

Salisbury

See palace: (1) aisled hall adjoining cathedral in Old Sarum; (2) a courtyard house set within the royal castle with its own hall and recalling the arrangement in Old Sherborne Castle, Dorset, also Bishop Roger's project; (3) the much altered palace of Bishop Poore built when the city was transferred into the valley to its present site in the 1220s and recently described by RCHME, a much altered building although one may suggest that the original hall of B. Poore was the 'solar' of the Commission. Discussion in the text (see p. 54) (RCHME, *City of Salisbury*, 1 and *City of Salisbury, 2, Houses in the Close*). Close and city licensed in 1328

London house: 'The next is Salisbury Court, a place so called, for that it belonged to the Bishops of Salisbury, and was their Inne or London house at such time as they were summoned to come to Parliament;' (Stow, 437). On Fleet Street between St Brides and Whitefriars with a river frontage. Licence for house Fleet Street 1337, repeated 1377. Site acquired 1194, Schofield, no. 79

Manor castles: Devizes, Wilts. 'Such a pecee of castle worke so costly and so strong was never before or since set up by any Bisshope' (Leland, 5, 82). An earlier castle enlarged by Bishop Roger (1103–39) who probably created the borough (Stone, 1920; *VCH*, 10, 243)

Kidwelly castle, Carmarthen. B. Roger acquired this place in S Wales in 1106, and constructed a castle there with an attached borough, well-preserved earthworks with later, non-episcopal masonry on top. This was perhaps the prototype for B. Roger's English castles (Fox and Radford, 1935)

Malmesbury, Wilts. B. Roger's castle now vanished

*Sherborne, Dorset. The most remarkable of B. Roger's castles on account of the design, a regular polygonal curtain with gatehouses with four-range inner courtyard with keep, claustrally inspired. The regularity and purposefulness of the design surprises. Confiscated at the end of Roger's life it was restored to the bishopric in the 14th century. Licence 1337, repeated 1377 (RCHME, 1, 66)

Manor houses: the six principal manors were licensed in 1337, confirmed 1377

Bishops Cannings, Wilts
*Bishops Woodford, Wilts
Chardstock, Devon
Cumnor, Berks
Edington, Wilts
Potterne, Wilts. Encaustic tiles found but bishop's house not firmly located (McGlashen and Sandall, 1974)
*Ramsbury, Wilts

*Sonning, Berks. A very remarkable excavation by Brakspear (1916) revealed on the N what was evidently the earlier 13th-century hall set over an undercroft, retained as a chamber when a larger hall was added at right angles and a courtyard with gatehouse was created on the W side

Winchester

See palace: instead of the usual westerly position the palace lay SE of the cathedral separated from the close by a stream. Two 12th-century bishops, Giffard and Henry of Blois, are responsible for most of what we see: the long range of the W hall raised on a chalk filling and the E hall partly aisled. The relationship of the curious 'protokeep' on the E side, or even its date remains unresolved. A gateway linked the two halls on the N side and there was a chapel between them on the S side. (Biddle, 1986)

London house: Winchester House on the Thames in Southwark. Now attributed to B. Henry of Blois mid-12th century, still the earliest London episcopal house. Long hall block of c. 1190 over vault, chamber division, three service doors below rose window in gable (Carlin, 1985). Schofield, no. 193

Manor castles: five castles founded by B. Henry of Blois in c. 1138 and slighted by the king in 1155

*Bishops Waltham, Hants. Rectangular moated enclosure (outer enclosure to N – ?failed borough – with excavated earlier buildings) with keep in one corner mainly from later work of Henry. Massive reconstruction by Wykeham and Beaufort in later period on evidence of manorial accounts. Long lodging range at N end, of which three units survive. Started life as castle but became a 'right ample and goodly maner place motid aboute' (Leland, 1, 285) very extensively used by the bishops (Lewis, 1985; Hare, 1987 and 1988)

Downton, Wilts. Earthworks survive from castle which never seems to have recovered from 1155 demolition but the bishop had residence there

*Farnham, Surrey. Triangular motte and bailey within a larger walled area. Spectacularly constructed motte enclosing stone tower enlarged at surface although superstructure probably demolished in 1155. Two periods of hall in 12th century, chapel, massive brick entry tower by Waynflete and much work at Restoration (*VCH*, 2, 599–605; Thompson, 1960, 1961)

Merdon, Hants. Perhaps a failed borough associated but had longer life than Downton. Impressive earthworks and also masonry of curtain and ?keep. (*VCH*, 3, 418; Thompson, 1966)

Taunton, Som. No doubt intended to enhance borough. Keep (?encased motte below) and two stages of hall in inner ward. Gateway to outer ward survives (Radford and Hallason, 1952)

Manor houses: for associated parks and fishponds see Roberts, 1986 and 1988

Alresford, Hants (*VCH*, 314–5)

Bishops Sutton, Hants

Bitterne, Hants. According to Leland 'sumtyme a castelle' (1, 280) but then a farm of the bishop. Remains of the manor house survive within the Roman shore fort of Clausentum at Southampton (Pevsner, 597)

East Meon, Hants. Opposite the fine Norman church the hall, 7.9 by 14.7 m, with solar over the low end, 5.5 by 11 m attached to a vanished but earlier upper end. Fine roof with kings' heads carved on corbels (Roberts, 1993)

*Esher, Surrey. Brick courtyard house of B. Wayneflete of which only the altered gatehouse survives (*VCH*, 3, 448–9)

Fareham, Hants (*VCH*, 3, 210–17)

*Highcleere, Hants (*VCH*, 4, 285–6)

Ivinghoe, Bucks (*VCH*, 379–80)

*Marwell, Owlesbury, Hants (*VCH*, 332–4)

[Rickmansworth, the More, Herts. Licence 1426. See Durham]

Wargrave, Berks

West Wycombe, Bucks (*VCH*, 136–7)

Witney, Oxon. A view by N. Buck in 1729 shows what appears to be a two-storeyed hall with pilasters. Excavations revealed a square stone structure with windows and central pier perhaps to support an open hearth on the first floor (cf. Eynsford, Kent) of a ?'protokeep' (Durham, 1985).

Worcester

See palace: licence for houses in close in close 1271. Encased in 18th-century exterior much of the medieval structure survives: four-bay undercroft of the hall and the chancel of the chapel (*VCH*, 306–7)

London house: After Lichfield 'next unto it and adjoyning was the Bishop of Worcesters Inne...' (Stow, 490a). In the Strand with river frontage but demolished for the construction of Somerset House in 1549

Manor castle: *Hartlebury, Worcs. Started by B. Cantilupe (1236–66) and finished by B. Giffard. Licence 1268 (not enrolled). Although largely rebuilt it retains its original shape of hall with cross wings. The original chapel in SW. A tower of the outer circuit survives at NW (*VCH*, 3, 381–3; *Arch. J.* (1995), 152, Supp., 37–9)

Manor houses: *Alvechurch, Worcs. Double moats on other side of river to church (*VCH*, 3, 381–3; Aston, 1972)

Bibury, Glos

Bishops Cleeve, Glos. Much altered but retains shape of hall with cross wings and three doorways at lower end of hall (Pevsner, 108)

Blockley, formerly Worcs now Glos. Manor house probably on site of episcopal residence. (*VCH*, 3, 266, 270). The Northwick of Leland (5, 228) which was moated and had a park was evidently this

*Bredon, Worcs. Tithe barn 36 m long with two porches (*VCH*, 279–81)

Fladbury, Worcs (*VCH*, 3, 352–4)

Hampton, Worcs?

Hampton Lucy, Warwicks (*VCH*, 3, 102–3)

Henbury in the Saltmarsh, Som. but formerly Glos

*Itchel (Ichull), Crondall, Hants, near Farnham, Surrey. London stop

*Kempsey, Worcs (*VCH*, 3, 430–2)

Ripple, Worcs (*VCH*, 3, 486–8)

*Weston Subedge, Glos

Wick Episcopi, Worcs (*VCH*, 3, 502)

*Withington, Glos. Licence 1271. Probably on site of present manor house. Ruinous in Leland's time (5, 228)

York

See palace: NW of cathedral. A short length of 12th-century arcade and a two-storeyed chapel of 1220–40 are all that survive (*VCH, City of York*, 340–1 with plan; detailed study by Butler, 1988)

London house: Wolsey's new building in York Place was taken over by Henry VIII for Whitehall Palace but plans of Wolsey's and earlier buildings have been recovered by excavation (Thurley, 1991). The Ab. moved into the adjoining plot that had belonged to the B. of Norwich

Manor castle: *Cawood, Yorks. Licence 1272. 'a very fair castel longging to the Archbishop of York' according to Leland (4, 12). Due to demolition by Parliament only Ab. Kempe's gatehouse of the mid-15th century survives. The adjoining canal for transporting stone from the Sherburn quarries and the gardens have been studied (Blood and Taylor, 1992)

Beverley, Yorks, ER

Bishop Burton, Yorks, ER

Bishopthorpe, Yorks. The present residence of the Ab. of York. Bought by Ab. Grey in 1241 who probably built the chapel which lies transversely across the lower end of the hall thereby preventing development and confining it to the upper end. The hall itself was two-storeyed and is infilled. The intricate history of the building was worked out with great skill by the late Dr Gee (1983)

Bishop Wilton, Yorks, ER

Hampton Court, Middx. Wolsey's palace (Thurley, 1991).

Hexham, the Archbishop's Precinct, Northumb. (Emery, 1, 101–2)

Kinoulton, Notts

Laneham, Notts. Abandoned by 15th century

Little Compton, formerly Glos., now Warwicks. Licence 1291. The Ab. did not own this parish but Condicote to W

Otley, Yorks, WR. Extreme W manor. Excavation revealed a two-storeyed chapel with apse subsequently extended W in a range (cf. Durham). It was only slightly used in the 13th century and went out of use in the following one (Le Patourel, 1973)

Oxton, Tadcaster

Rest Park, Yorks, WR. Licence 1383 to erect fortlet. Excavation revealed continuous ranges within the moats but not very robust structures (Le Patourel, 1973a)

Ripon, Yorks, WR

Sherburn in Elmet, York, WR

Scrooby, Notts. Two courts in brick and timber according to Leland (1, 34)

Southwell, Notts. Present bishop has modern house but extensive remains exist of medieval Ab.'s house begun by Ab. Thoresby in 1360 and completed in 1430. Faulkner has worked out plan (1970, 130–2). The building is well-known for its latrine with radial seats in corner tower (Gill, 1906)

[Rickmansworth, the More, Herts. Cardinal Wolsey undertook major building works there, enclosing the older work with new ranges all round but this was done as abbot of St Albans, not as Ab. of

York. Cf. earlier work done by Durham and Winchester (Thurley, 1991)]

Bibliography

This bibliography is in no sense exhaustive for the amount of material published, let alone unpublished, on bishops is boundless; it represents works consulted by myself, often but not always referred to in the text. It is divided into contemporary and modern works, although I suppose in some sense material remains of the period are as contemporary as written ones.

A. Contemporary sources

Arnold, T. (ed.) (1885), *Simeon of Durham*, RS.

Barley, M. W., Stevenson, W. H. and Cameron, K. (eds) (1956), *Documents Relating to the Manor and Soke of Newark*, Nottingham.

Bosanquet, G. (ed.) (1964), *Eadmer's History of Recent Events in England*, London.

Brewer, T. S. and Martin, C. T. (eds) (1880), *Registrum Malmesburiense*, 2 vols, RS.

Chibnall, M. (ed.) (1969), *The Ecclesiastical History of Orderic Vitalis*, vol. 2, Oxford.

Colvin, H. M. and Foster, S. (eds) (1996), *The Panorama of London circa 1544 by Anthonis van den Wyngaerde*, London.

Crosby, J. H. (1889–1914), *Ely Episcopal Registers (1337–1581)*.

Davis, F. N. (ed.) (1913), *Rotuli Roberti Grosseste*, CYS.

———, Foster, C. W. and Thompson, A. H. (eds) (1925), *Rotuli Ricardi Gravesend diocesis Lincolnienses*, CYS.

Deedes, C. (ed.) (1905), 'Extracts from the episcopal register of Bishop Praty (1438–45)', SRS, 4, 85–61.

———(ed.) (1908), 'The episcopal register of Robert Rede, 1397–1415', SRS, 8, 11 (two parts).

Dimock, J. F. (ed.) (1877), *Giraldi Cambrensis, Vita S. Remigii et vita S. Hugonis*, vol. 7, RS.

Douie, D. L. and Farmer, H. (ed.) (1962), *The Life of St Hugh of Lincoln*, London.

Dunstan, G. R. (ed.) (1963), *The Register of Edmund Lacy, Bishop of Exeter 1420–55*, CYS.

Foster, C. W. (ed.) (1931), *Registrum Antiquissimum of the Cathedral Church of Lincoln*, vol. 1, Lincolnshire Record Society, 27.

Galbraith, V. N. (ed.) (1927), *The Anonimaille Chronicle*, Manchester.

Goodman, A. W. (ed.) (1940), *Registrum Henrici Woodlock, diocesis Wintoniensis, AD 1035–16*, CYS.

Graham, R. (ed.) (1952), *Registrum Roberti Winchelsey, Cantuarensis, AD 1295–1313*, CYS.

Griffiths, M. A. and Capes, W. W. (eds) (1907), *Registrum Thome de Cantilupe episcopi Herefordensis, AD MCCLXXV–MCCLXXXII*, CYS.

Hall, II. (ed.) (1903), *The Pipe Roll of the bishopric of Winchester, 1208–09*, London.

Hamilton, N. E. S. A. (ed.) (1870), *William of Malmesbury, De gestis pontificum Anglorum*, RS.

Hardy, T. D. (ed.) (1873–8), *Registrum palatii Dunelmense: the Register of Bishop Richard de Kellonde, 1311–16*, 4 vols, RS.

Harvey, J. H. (ed.) (1969), *William Worcestre: Itineraries*, Oxford.

Hobhouse, E. (ed.) (1887), *Calendar of the Register of John de Drokensford, Bishop of Bath and Wells, 1309–29*, Somerset Records Society.

Hudson, W. and Tingey, J. C. (eds) (1906), *The Records of the City of Norwich*, 2 vols, Norwich.

Jacob, E. F. (ed.) (1943), *The Register of Henry Chichele, Archbishop of Canterbury, 1414–43*, CYS.

Johnson, C. (ed.) (1948), *Registrum Hamonis Hethe, diocensis Roffensis, AD 1319–52*, CYS.

Luard, E. (ed.) (1851), *Roberti Grosseteste episcopi....epistolae*, RS.

— (1864), *Annales monastici, Annales Wintoniae*, vol. 2, RS.

Oschinsky, D. (ed.) (1971), *Walter of Henley and Other Treatises on Estate Management and Accounting*, Oxford.

Page, M. (ed.) (1996), *The Pipe Roll of the Bishopric of Winchester, 1301–2*, Winchester.

Palmer, T. F. (ed.) (1924), 'The household roll of Bishop Ralph of Shrewsbury (1337–8)', *Somerset Rec. Soc.*, 39, 72–174.

Peckham, W. D. (ed.) (1925) in 'Thirteen Ciistumals of the Sussex manor of the bishop of Chichester', *SRS*, 31.

Pobst, P. E. (ed.) (1996), *The Register of William Bateman, Bishop of Norwich, 1344–55*, CYS.

Potter, K. R. (ed.) (1955), *The Historia Novella by William of Malmesbury*, London.

——(1955a), *Gesta Stephani*, London.

Powell, E. and Trevelyan, G. M. (eds) (1899), *The Peasants' Rising and the Lollards: a Collection of Unpublished Documents*, London.

Pryce, A. I. (ed.) (1922), 'The Register of Benedict, bishop of Bangor, 1408–17', *Archaeologia Cambrensis*, 97, 80–108.

— (1923), *The Diocese of Bangor in the Sixteenth Century: a Digest of the Registers of the Bishops 1512–1646*, Bangor.

Raine, J. (ed.) (1839), *Historiae Dunelmensis Scriptores Tres*, Surtees Society.

Roberts, R. A. (ed.) (1920), *The Episcopal Registers of the Diocese of St Davids, 1397–1518*, Cymmrodorion Record Series, 6.

Rogers, J. E. T. (ed.) (1881), *Locie libro veritatum, by Thomas Gascoigne, 1403–1458*, Oxford.

— (ed.) (1891), *Oxford City Documents*, Oxford.

Smith, L. T. (ed.) (1964), *The Itinerary of John Leland* (reprint), London.

Southern, R. W. (ed. and trans.) (1962), Eadmer: *The life of Anselm, Archbishop of Canterbury*, Oxford.

Storey, R. L. (ed.) (1995), *The Register of John Kirkby, Bishop of Carlisle, 1332–52, and the Register of John Ross*, 2 vols, CYS.

Stow, J. (1633), *The Survey of London*, 3rd. edn, London.

Taxatio ecclesiastica Angliae et Walliae auctoritate P. Nicolai IV, c. 1291, Record Commission, 1802.

Timmins, T. C. B. (ed.) (1994), *The Register of John Waltham, Bishop of Salisbury, 1388–95*, CYS.

Tynedale, W. (1530), 'The practice of prelates' in H. Walter (ed.), *Expositions and Notes*, Cambridge, 1849.

Valor Ecclesiasticus (1810–34), 6 vols, Record Commission.

Walberg, E. (ed.) (1922), *La vie de Saint Thomas le Martyr par Guernes de Pont-Saint-Maxence, poeme historique du XIIe siecle (1172–74)*, Lund.

Webb, J. (ed.) (1853, 1855), *A Roll of the Household Expenses of Richard de Swinfield, Bishop Hereford during Parts of the Years 1289, 1290*, 2 vols, Camden Society.

Willis-Bund, J. W. (ed.) (1902), *Episcopal Register of Bishop Godfrey Giffard, September 1268–August 1301*, 2 vols, Worcestershire Archaeological Society.

Wilson, R. A., (ed.) (1905, 1907), *The Registers or Act Books of the Bishops of Coventry and Lichfield: the Second Register of Bishop*

Robert de Stretton AD 1368–85, William Salt Archaeological Society.

Wright, D. P. (ed.) (1985), *The Register of Thomas Langton, Bishop of Salisbury, 1485–93*, CYS.

B.   Modern works

Aberth, J. (1996), *Criminal Churchmen in the age of Edward III: the Case of Thomas de Lisle*, Pennsylvania.

Adams, K. A. (1990), 'Monastery and village at Crayke, North Yorkshire', *YAJ*, 62, 29–60.

Alcock, N. W. (1966), 'The medieval buildings at Bishops Clyst', *Reports and Transactions of the Devonshire Association*, 98, 132–55.

Anderson, J. C. (1882), *A Short Chronicle concerning the parish of Croydon*, London.

Aston, M. (1967), *Thomas Arundel: a Study of Church Life in the Reign of Richard II*, Oxford.

——(1972), 'Earthworks of the Bishop's Palace, Alvechurch, Worcestershire', *Trans. Worcs. Arch. Soc.*, 13, 55–9.

Atherton, L., Fence, F., Harper-Bill, C. and Smith, H. (eds) (1996), *Norwich Cathedral: Church, City and Diocese, 1096–1996*, London.

Atkinson, T.D. (1943), 'Winchester Cathedral close', *PHFCAS*, 15, 9–26.

Barlow, F. (1986), *Thomas Becket*, London.

Barron, C. M. and Harper-Bill, C. (eds) (1955), *The church in pre-Reformation Society: Essays in Honour of F. P. H. Du Boulay*, Woodbridge.

Bellamy, J. G. (1964), 'The Coterel gang: an anatomy of a band of fourteenth century criminals', *EHR*, 79, 698–717.

——(1973), *Crime and Public Order in England in the Later Middle Ages*, London.

Beresford, M. (1959), 'The six new towns of the bishops of Winchester', *MA*, 3, 187–215.

——(1967), *New Towns of the Middle Ages*, London.

——and Finsberg, H. P. R. (1973), *English Medieval Boroughs: a Handlist*, Totowa.

Bevan, W. C. (1888), *Diocesan Histories: St Davids*, London.

Biddle, M. (1986), *Wolvesey Old Bishop's Palace, Winchester*, London.

——, Barfield, L. and Millard, A. (1959), 'The excavation of the manor of the More, Rickmansworth, Hertfordshire', *AJ*, 116, 136–99.

Bilson, J. (1915), 'The manor house of the bishops of Durham at Howden', *YAJ*, 22, 256–69.

Blair, J. (1987), 'The twelfth-century bishop's palace at Hereford', *MA*, 31, 59–71.

——(1993), 'Hall and chamber: English domestic planning 1000–1250' in G. Meirion-Jones, J. Blair and P. Dixon (eds), *Manorial domestic buildings in England and northern France*, London.

Blaylock, S. (1990), 'The Bishop's Palace' [at Exeter], *AJ*, 147, Supp. 41–5.

Blood, N. K. and Taylor, C. C. (1992), 'Cawood: an archiepiscopal landscape', *YAJ*, 64, 83–102.

Bradfer-Lawrence, H. L. (1932), 'Gaywood Dragge', *Norfolk Archaeology*, 24, 146–83.

Brakspear, H. (1916), 'The bishop's palace, Sonning', *Berks, Bucks and Oxon Archaeological J.*, 22, 7–21.

——(1933), 'The abbot's house at Battle', *Arch.*, 83, 139–66.

Braun, H. (1935), 'Notes on Newark castle', *Trans. Thoroton Society of Notts*, 39, 53–91.

Braunfels, W. (1972), *Urban Design in Western Europe: Regime and Architecture, 900–1000*, Chicago.

Brett, M. (1975), *The English Church under Henry I*, Oxford.

Brooks, C. (1990), 'Bishops Court, Devon', *Country Life*, 184 (7), 54–8.

Brown, R. A. (1959), 'A list of castles, 1154–1216', *EHR*, 74, 249–80.

Bruhl C. (1974), 'Konigs-, Bischofs- and Stadtpfalz in dem Stadten des Regnum Italiae vom 9 bis zum 13 Jahrhundert', in H. Beumann, *Historische Forschungen fur Walter Schlesinger*, Cologne, 400–20.

Buckle, E. (1888), 'Wells palace', *PSANHS*, 34, 54–97.

Butler, R. M. (1988), 'York Place, a vanished Jacobean mansion', *York Historian*, 8, 25–41.

Carlin, M. (1985), 'The reconstruction of Winchester house', *London Topographical Record*, 25, 35–57.

Chanter, J. F. (1932), *The Bishop's Palace at Exeter*, Exeter.

Chapman, H., Coppack, G. and Drewett, P. (1975), 'Excavations at the bishop's palace, Lincoln', *Occasional Papers in Lincolnshire History and Archaeology* I (whole issue).

Chapman, M., Davenport, P. and Holland, E. (1995), 'The precincts of the bishop's palace at Bath, Avon', *AJ*, 152, 95–109.

Cheney, C. R. (1941), *English Synodalia of the Thirteenth Century*, Oxford.

Cheney, M. G. (1980), *Roger, Bishop of Worcester, 1164–1179*, Oxford.

Coleman, M. C. (1984), *Downham-in-the-Isle*, Woodbridge.

Coulson, C. L. H. (1982), *Handlist of Royal Licences to Crenellate, 1200–78*, (handwritten list).

Cunningham, J. (1990), 'Auckland castle: some recent discoveries' in E. Fernie and P. Crossley (eds), *Medieval Architecture and its Intellectual Context*, London, 81–90.

Curnow, P. E. and Thompson, M. W. (1969), 'Excavations at Richards Castle, Herefordshire, 1962–64', *JBAA*, 3rd ser., 32, 105–27.

Davis, V. (1993), *William Wayneflete: Bishop and Educationalist*, Woodbridge.

Dixon, P. and Marshall, P. (1993), 'The great tower in the twelfth century: the case of Norham castle', *AJ*, 150, 410–32.

Du Boulay, P. R. H. (1950), 'A note on the rebuilding of Knole by Archbishop Bourgchier', *AC*, 63, 135–9.

——(1960), 'The Archbishop as a territorial magnate', *Medieval Records of the Archbishop of Canterbury*, London, 50–70.

——(1966), *The Lordship of Canterbury: an Essay on Medieval Society*, London.

Dunning, R. W. (1966), 'The households of the bishops of Bath and Wells in the later middle ages', *PSANHS*, 110, 24–39.

Durham, B. (1985), *Witney Palace, Excavations at Mount House, Witney, in 1984*, Oxford.

Edwards, K. (1949), 'The houses of Salisbury close in the fourteenth century', *JBAA*, 3rd ser., 4, 55–115.

——(1949), *The English Secular Cathedrals in the Middle Ages*, Manchester.

Emery, A. H. (1994), 'Saltwood castle', *AJ*, 151, Supp., 30–4.

——(1996), *Greater Medieval Houses of England and Wales: 1, Northern England*, vols 2 and 3 forthcoming, Cambridge.

Emsley, K. (1975), 'The Yorkshire enclaves of the bishop of Durham, *YAJ*, 47, 103–8.

Esquieu, Y. and Pradalier, H. (1996), 'Les palais épiscopaux dans la

France meridionale' in A. Renoux (ed.), *Palais royaux et princiers au moyen age*, University of Maine.

Evans, E. (1983), *Swansea Castle and the Medieval Town*, Swansea.

Evans, W. (1991), *St Davids Bishop's Palace*, Cadw, Cardiff.

Faulkner, P. A. (1970), 'Some medieval archiepiscopal palaces', *AJ*, 127, 130–46.

——(1974), 'Lincoln Old Bishop's Palace', *AJ*, 131, 140–4.

Fox, C. and Radford, C. A. R. (1935), 'Kidwelly castle, Carmarthenshire, including a survey of polychrome pottery', *Arch.*, 83, 93–138.

Frazer, C. M. (1957), *A History of Anthony Bek, Bishop of Durham, 1283–1311*, Oxford.

Fryde, E. B., Greenway, D. E., Porter, S. and Roy, I. (eds) (1986), *Handbook of British Chronology*, 3rd edn, London.

Gee, E. A. (1983), *Bishopthorpe Palace*, York.

——and Miller, J. S. (1983), 'The Bishop Dyke and Huddleston Quarry', *YAJ*, 55, 167.

Gill, H. (1906), 'The palace, Southwell', *Trans. Thoroton Soc.*, 10, 73–5.

Gough, N. R. (1890), 'The archiepiscopal palace and chapel, Croydon', *Trans. St Paul's Ecclesiological Soc.*, 2, 41–3.

Greenwell, W. (1934), 'The early history of Durham castle', *Trans. Archit. Archaeol. Soc. of Durham and Northumberland*, 7 (1), 56–9.

Gunn, S. J. and Lindley, P. G. (eds) (1991), *Wolsey: Church, State and Art*, Cambridge.

Hannah, I. C. (1909), 'The bishop's palace, Chichester', *SAC*, 52, 1–23.

Hare, J. N. (1987), *Bishops Waltham Palace*, English Heritage.

——(1988), 'Bishops Waltham Palace, Hampshire: William of Wykeham, Henry Beaufort and the transformation of a medieval episcopal palace', *AJ*, 145, 222–54.

Hasler, J. and Luker, B. (1994), 'The site of the bishop's palace, Wookey', *PSANHS*, 137, 111–22.

Hasted, E. (1797–1801), *The History of the County of Kent*, 12 vols.

Heal, F. (1980), *Of Prelates and Princes: a Study of the Economic and Social Position of the Tudor Episcopate*, Cambridge.

Héliot, P. (1976), 'Nouvelles remarques sur les palais episcopaux de l'epoque romane en France', *Francia*, 4, 194–212.

Hembry, P. (1967), *The Bishops of Bath and Wells, 1540–1640: Social and Economic Problems*, London.

——(1978), 'Episcopal palaces, 1535–1660' in R. J. Krech, J. T. Scarisbrook and E. W. Ives, (eds), *Wealth and Power in Tudor England*, London, 146–66.

Hesketh, C. (1915), 'The manor house and great park of the archbishop of Canterbury at Otford', *AC*, 31, 1–24.

Hill, G. (1900), *English Dioceses*, London.

Hill, J. W. F. (1930), 'Lincoln castle, the constables and the guard', *Rep. and Pap. of the Archit. Soc. of Lincoln*, 40.

Hilton, R. H. (1973), *Bond Men Made Free: Medieval Peasant Movements and the English Rising of 1381*, London.

——(1990), *English Class Conflict and the Crisis of Feudalism*, London.

——(1996), *A Medieval Society, the West Midlands at the End of the Thirteenth Century*, London.

——and Ashton, T. (eds) (1984), *The English Rising of 1381*, London.

Hodgson, J. F. (1896), 'The chapel of Auckland castle', *Archaeologia Aeliana*, 18, 113–240.

Hope, W. St J. (1900), *The Architectural History of the Cathedral Church and Monastery of St Andrew at Rochester*, London.

Howell, M. (1982), 'Abbatial vacancies and the divided mensa in medieval England', *J. Eccles. Hist.* 33, 173–92.

Hunter-Blair, C. H. and Honeyman, H. L. (1966), *Norham Castle, Northumberland*, HMSO.

Hussey, C. (1928), 'Ely Palace, Cambridgeshire', *Country Life*, 63, 850–7.

——(1942), 'Saltwood castle', *Country Life*, 92, 986–9, 1034–7, 1082–5.

Johns, C. N. (1974), 'The castle and manor of Llandaff', *Glamorgan Historian*, 10, 172–95.

Jones, W. B. J. and Freeman, E. A. (1856), *The History and Antiquities of St Davids*, London.

Judd, A. (1961), *The Life of Thomas Bekynton*, Chichester.

Kealey, E. J. (1972), *Roger of Salisbury, Viceroy of England*, Berkeley.

Kershaw, S. W. (1914), 'The archbishop's manors in Sussex', *JBAA*, New Ser., 107–14.

Kettle, A. S. (1985), 'City and close: Lichfield in the century before the Reformation', in C. M. Barron and C. Harper-Bill (eds), *The Church in pre-Reformation Society*, Woodbridge, 158–70.

Kingsford, C. L. (1922), 'Bath Inn or Arundel House', *Arch.*, 72, 243–77.

Kipps, P. K. (1934), 'The palace of the archbishops of Canterbury at Charing, Kent', *AJ*, 90, 78–97.

Kissan, B. W. (1939), 'Lanfranc's alleged division of lands between archbishop and community', *EHR*, 54, 285–93.

Knowles, M. D. (1961), 'The English bishops 1070–1532' in J. A. Watt, J. B. Morrell and F. X. Martin (eds), *Medieval Studies*, Dublin.

Laithwaite, M., Blaylock, S. R. and Westcott, R. A. (1989), 'The bishop's palace at Bishopsteighton', *Proc. Devon Arch. Soc.*, 47, 53–69.

Le Patourel, J. (1973), *The Moated Sites of Yorkshire*, London.

Le Patourel, J. and Wood, P. (1973), 'Excavation of the Archbishop of York's manor house at Otley', *YAJ*, 45, 115–41.

Lewis, E. (1985), 'Excavations in Bishops Waltham', 1967–78', *PHFCAS*, 41, 81–125.

Leyland, M. (1994), 'The origins and development of Durham castle' in D. Rollason, M. Harvey and M. Prestwich (eds), *Anglo-Norman Durham, 1093–1193*, Woodbridge, 407–24.

Lilley, K. D. (1994), 'Coventry's topographical development: the impact of the Priory' in G. Demidowicz, *Coventry's first cathedral*, Stamford, 72–96.

Lobel, M. D. (1969), *Historic Towns*, vols 1 and 2, London.

Maddison, J. (1993), 'Building at Lichfield during the episcopate of Walter Langton (1296–1321)' in J. Maddison (ed.), *Medieval Archaeology and Architecture in Lichfield*, 65–84.

Marshall, P. and Samuels, J. (1997), *Guardian of the Trent: the Story of Newark Castle*, Newark.

McGlashan, N. D. and Sandall, R. E. (1974), 'The bishop of Salisbury's house at his manor of Potterne', *Wilts. Arch. and Nat. Hist. Mag.*, 69, 85–96.

Mecksepert, C. (1986), 'Das Palatium Ottes des Grossen in Magdeburg', *Burgen und Schlosser*, 27, 101–5.

Meirion-Jones, G. (1969), 'Dogmersfield and Hastley Maudit: two deserted villages', *PHFCAS*, 26, 111–27.

Mertes, K. (1988), *The English Noble Household, 1250–1600*, Oxford.

Miller, E. (1951), *The Abbey and Bishopric of Ely*, Cambridge.

Miller, M. C. (1995), 'From episcopal to Communal palaces: palaces and power in northern Italy 1000–1250', *J. Soc. Archit. Historians*, 54/2, 175–85.

Moorman, J. R. H. (1945), *Church Life in England in the Thirteenth Century*, Cambridge.

Mortet, V. (1888), *Étude historique et archéologique sur la cathedrale et le palais episcopal de Paris du VIᵉ au XIIᵉ siecle*, Paris.

O'Neil, H. (1956), 'Prestbury Moat', *Trans. Bristol and Gloucester Arch. Soc.*, 75, 5–34.

Packham, A. B. (1923), 'The "Old Palace" at West Tarring', *SAC*, 64, 140–80.

Parker, J. II. (1863), 'The bishop's palace at Wells', *PSANHS*, 143–58.

Pearman, A. I., Tait, G. H. and Thompson, H. P., 1918, 'Residences of the bishops of Rochester', *AC*, 33, 131–54.

Peckham, W. D. (1921), 'The architectural history of Amberley castle', *SAC*, 62, 21–63.

Pike, L. O. (1873–6), *A History of Crime in England*, 2 vols, London.

Powell, E., 1896, *The Rising in East Anglia in 1381*, Cambridge.

Pryor, E. A. (n.d.), *Nursestead Court*.

Radford, C. A. R. (1948), *The Bishop's Palace at Lamphey, Pembrokeshire*, HMSO.

——(1955), *The Bishop's Palace, St Davids, Pembrokeshire*, HMSO.

——(1961), 'Acton Burnell castle', in E. M. Jope (ed.), *Studies in Building History*, London, 94–103.

——and Hallason, A. B. (1952), 'The history of Taunton castle in the light of recent discoveries', *PSANHS*, 98, 55–98.

Rady, J., Tatton-Brown, T. and Bowen, J. A. (1991), 'The archbishop's palace, Canterbury', *JBAA*, 144, 1–60.

Raine, J. (1852), *A Brief Historical Account of the Episcopal Castle or Palace of Auckland*, Durham.

Raine, J. (the younger) (1876), 'Survey of the manor house of Stockton, commonly called Stockton castle, taken after the death of Bishop Pilkington', *Archaeologia Aeliana*, 7, 120–5.

Rendell, I. M. (1963), 'Blackford (Wedmore), the bishop's palace', *PSANHS*, 107, 71–8.

Reynolds, N. (1975), 'Investigations in the Observatory Tower, Lincoln castle, *NA*, 19, 201–5.

Riall, N. (1994), *Henry of Blois, Bishop of Winchester: a Patron of the Twelfth Century Renaissance*, Winchester.

Richardson, R. K. (1913), 'The bishopric of Durham under Anthony Bek, 1283–1311' *Archaeologia Aeliana*, 3rd ser., 10, 89–229.

Rigold, S. E. (1963), 'The Anglian cathedral of North Elmham, Norfolk', *MA*, 6/7, 67–108.

——(1989), 'Maidstone: the archiepiscopal precinct', *AJ*, 126, 252–4.

Roberts, E. (1867), 'On Mayfield in Sussex', *JBAA*, 23, 33–59.

——(1986), 'The bishop of Winchester's fishponds in Hampshire, 1150–1400: their development, function and management' *PHFCAS*, 42, 123–38.

——(1988), 'The bishop of Winchester's deer parks in Hampshire, 1200–1400', *PHFCAS*, 44, 67–85.

——(1993), 'William of Wykeham's house at East Meon', *AJ*, 150, 433–55.

——(1993a), 'The bishop of Winchester's fishponds and deerparks', *PHFCAS*, 49, 229–31.

Rodwell, K. A. (1976), 'Excavations on the site of Banbury castle, 1973–4', *Oxoniensa*, 41, 90–148.

Rye, W. B. (1887), 'The ancient episcopal palace at Rochester and Bishop Fisher', *AC*, 17, 66–76.

Salmon, J. (n.d.), *Acton Burnell and its Church*.

Saunders, A. D. (1971), *Barnard Castle*, HMSO.

Saxl, F. (1947), 'Lincoln cathedral: the eleventh century design for the west front', *AJ*, 103, 105–18.

Scammel, G. V. (1956), *Hugh du Puiset, Bishop of Durham*, Cambridge.

Schulz, J. (1982), 'The Communal buildings of Parma', *Mitteilungen des Kunsthistorisches Institutes in Florenz*, 26, 279–323.

Schofield, J. (1995), *Medieval London Houses*, London.

Simpson, W. D. (1961), *The Castles of Bergen and the Bishop's Palace at Kirkwall*, Edinburgh.

Simpson, W. S. (1905), 'The palaces or town houses of the bishops of London', *TLMAS*, 13–71.

Smith, P. (1975), *Houses of the Welsh Countryside*, Cardiff.

Stevenson, F. S. (1899), *Robert Grosseteste, Bishop of Lincoln*, London.

Stewart-Brown, R. (1936), *The Sergeants of the Peace in Medieval England and Wales*, Manchester.

Stone, E. H. (1920), *Devizes Castle: its History and Romance*, Devizes.

Tait, R. S. (1910), *Episcopal Palaces (Province of Canterbury)*, London.

Tatham, G. B. (1908), 'The sale of episcopal lands during the Civil Wars and Commonwealth', *EHR*, 23, 91–108.

Tatton-Brown, T. (1984), 'Three great Benedictine Houses in Kent: their buildings and topography', *AC*, 100, 171–8.

Taylor, C. C. (1989), 'Somersham palace: a medieval landscape for pleasure?', *Brit. Arch. Rep.*, 209, 211–24.

——(1989a), 'Spaldwick, Cambridgeshire', *Proc. Cambs. Ant. Soc.*, 78, 76–82.

Thompson, A. H. (1925), *The Cathedral Churches of England*, London.

——(1927), *The Medieval Bishops in their Dioceses*, York Minster Tract.

——(1933), 'William Bateman, bishop of Norwich', *AJ*, 90.

——(1945), 'Thomas Langley, Bishop of Durham, 1406–37', *Durham University Journal*, 38.

——(1947), *The English Clergy and their Organisation in the Later Middle Ages*, Oxford.

——(1952), 'William Alnwick, bishop of Lincoln', *AJ*, 106, Supp., 98–112.

Thompson, M. W. (1960), 'Recent excavations in the keep of Farnham castle, Surrey', *MA*, 4, 81–94.

——(1960a), 'The date of "Fox's tower", Farnham castle, Surrey', *Surrey Arch. Coll.*, 57, 85–92.

——(1961), *Farnham Castle Keep, Surrey*, HMSO.

——(1966), 'Merdon castle', *AJ*, 123, 221.

——(1987), *The Decline of the Castle*, Cambridge.

——(1991), *The Rise of the Castle*, Cambridge.

——(1994), 'The place of Durham among Norman episcopal palaces and castles', in D. Rollason, M. Harvey and M. Prestwich (eds), *Anglo-Norman Durham, 1093–1193*, Woodbridge.

——(1995), *'The Medieval Hall: the Basis of Secular Domestic Life, 600–1600 AD*, Aldershot.

——(1995a), 'Another "proto-keep" at Walmer, Kent', *MA*, 174–6.

——(1998, forthcoming), 'The early topography of the castle', in P. Lindley (ed.), *Lincoln Castle*, London.

Thurley, S. (1991), 'The domestic building works of Cardinal Wolsey', in S. Gunn and P. Lindley (eds), *Cardinal Wolsey: Church State and Art*, Cambridge.

Toy, S. (1946), 'Winchester House, Southwark', *Surrey Arch. Coll.*, 49, 75–81.

Tringham, N. (1993), 'The palace of Bishop Walter Langton in Lichfield cathedral close', in J. Maddison (ed.), *Medieval Art and Architecture in Lichfield*, London.

Turner, R. (1991), *Lamphey Bishop's Palace: Llawhaden Castle*, Cadw. Cardiff.

Turner, T. H. and Parker, J. H. (1852–9), *Some Account of Domestic Architecture in England from the Conquest to Henry VIII*, 4 vols, Oxford.

Venables, E. (1895), *Episcopal Palaces of England*, London.

Voss, L. (1932), *Heinrich von Blois, Bischof von Winchester (1129–71)*, Historische Studien 210.

West, J. (1981), 'Acton Burnell castle, Shropshire' in A. Detsicas (ed.), *Collectanea Historica*, 85–92.

Whittingham, A. B. (1949), 'The monastic buildings of Norwich cathedral', *AJ*, 106, 86–7.

——(1980), 'The bishop's palace, Norwich', *AJ*, 37, 365–8.

Williams, G. (1981), 'Henry de Gower (?1278–1347), bishop and builder', *Archaeologia Cambrensis*, 130, 1–18.

Wilson, J. (1912), *Rose Castle: the Residential Seat of the Bishop of Carlisle*, Carlisle.

Wingfield, D. E. (1979), *Penryn: archaeology and development, a survey*, Truro.

Wood, C. P. (1975), 'Emergency excavations at Otford palace', *AC*, 89, 191–203.

Wood, M. (1965), *The English Medieval House*, London.

Woodfield, C. and P. (1981–2), 'The palace of the bishop of Lincoln at Lyddington', *Trans. Leics Arch. and Hist. Soc.*, 57, 1–16.

——(1988), *Lyddington Bede House*, London.

Woodman, F. (1981), *The Architectural History of Canterbury Cathedral*, Cambridge.

Yates, R. (1843), *History and Antiquities of the Abbey of St Edmundsbury*, 2nd edn, London.

Zotz, T. (1993), 'Carolingian tradition and Ottonian-Salian innovation: comparative observations on palatine policy in the Empire,' in A. J. Duggan (ed.), *Kings and Kingship in Medieval Europe*, London, 69–100.

Index

Bishop is abbreviated to B, Archbishop to Ab and bishop's palace to BP. Where there is an illustration the figure is in *italics*.